Ritual Abuse

WHAT IT IS, WHY IT HAPPENS,
AND HOW TO HELP

D0207362

Ritual Abuse

WHAT IT IS, WHY IT HAPPENS,
AND HOW TO HELP

Margaret Smith

HarperSanFrancisco
A Division of HarperCollins*Publishers*

FIRST EDITION

Library of Congress Cataloging-in-Publication Data

Smith, Margaret.
    Ritual abuse : what it is, why it happens, and how to help /
Margaret Smith. — 1st ed.
        p.   cm.
    Includes bibliographical references.
    ISBN 0-06-250214-X (acid-free paper)
    1. Child abuse—United States.   2. Adult child abuse victims—
United States.   3. Cults—United States.   4. Satanism—United
States.   I. Title.
HV6626.5.S56   1993
362.7′6—dc20   92–56420
                                                              CIP

93 94 95 96 97 RRD(H) 10 9 8 7 6 5 4 3 2 1

This edition is printed on acid-free paper that meets the American
National Standards Institute Z39.48 Standard.

Contents

Preface

If there is even a small chance that one ritual abuse claim is true, we owe it to all potential victims to explore the problem of ritual abuse in greater depth.

Why immediately discount those who say they were ritually abused when history reveals that religious and political obsession often leads to violence? Innocent women, children, and men were tortured during the Inquisition because of religious obsession. Adolf Hitler, in the name of political obsession, turned a whole country into a murdering nation by killing innocent Jews and other minority groups. Recently, near Waco, Texas, we once again saw how the obsessive spiritual beliefs of a group, led by David Koresh who said he was the second coming of Christ, led to violence. Ritual abuse survivors say they were violently abused in religious rituals by groups that were using them as magical tools or that were trying to indoctrinate them into the belief system of the group. They say the groups are extremely violent and secretive, and hence do not live in communal settings, as was the case in Waco, Texas. Are claims of ritual abuse really that bizarre after we reflect upon the historical acts of groups that were obsessed with religion and politics?

There is some truth to the claim that a few advocates for ritual abuse survivors have irresponsibly approached the topic of ritual abuse. Nevertheless, it is hasty to discount all accusations of ritual abuse merely because some advocates do not appear credible. It is not beyond the realm of possibilities that there are dangerous religious cults in our communities.

Four states have now passed laws specifically prohibiting ritual child abuse. A number of studies have been conducted that illustrate the marked similarities in abuse allegations of adult and child ritual abuse survivors. Convictions have been obtained in over ten court cases in which the children made allegations of ritual abuse. We need to know more about the problem. We need to know who the groups are and what are the belief systems of the people ritually abusing children. We need to know how prevalent the problem is. We need to know how to protect the children and how to help the adults heal. We need legislation to protect the victims. We need you to care.

As you read this book, you may find that some ritual abuse allegations are more difficult to believe than others. All we ask is that you believe what you can. If legislation is passed specifically prohibiting this type of criminal activity—and if our law enforcement officials are encouraged to investigate such cases—the activities of such groups will be revealed to the public.

Chapter 1

What Is Ritual Abuse?

Betrayal is too kind a word to describe a situation in which a father says he loves his daughter, but claims he must teach her about the horrors of the world in order to make her a stronger person; a situation in which he watches or participates in rituals that make her feel like she is going to die. She experiences pain that is so intense that she cannot think; her head spins so fast she can't remember who she is or how she got there.

All she knows is pain. All she feels is desperation. She tries to cry out for help, but soon learns that no one will listen. No matter how loud she cries, she can't stop or change what is happening. No matter what she does, the pain will not stop. Her father orders her to be tortured and tells her it is for her own good. He tells her that she needs the discipline, or that she has asked for it by her misbehavior. Betrayal is too simple a word to describe the overwhelming pain, the overwhelming loneliness and isolation this child experiences.

As if the abuse during the rituals were not enough, this child experiences similar abuse at home on a daily basis. When she tries to talk about her pain, she is told that she must be crazy. "Nothing bad has happened to you," her family tells her. Each day she begins to feel more and more like she doesn't know what is real. She stops trusting her own feelings because no one else acknowledges them or hears her agony. Soon the pain becomes too great. She learns not to feel at all. This strong, lonely, desperate child learns to give up the senses that make all people feel alive. She begins to feel dead. She wishes she were dead. For her, there is no way out. She soon learns there is no hope.

As she grows older, she gets stronger. She learns to do what she is told with the utmost compliance. She forgets everything she has ever wanted. The pain still lurks, but it's easier to pretend it's not there than to acknowledge the horrors she has buried in the deepest parts of her mind. Her relationships are overwhelmed by the power of her emotions. She reaches out for help, but never seems to find what she is looking for. The pain gets worse. The loneliness sets in. When the feelings return, she is overcome with panic, pain, and desperation. She is convinced she is going to die. Yet, when she looks around her, she sees nothing that should make her feel so bad. Deep inside she knows something is very, very wrong, but she doesn't remember anything. She thinks, "Maybe I am crazy."

The State of Illinois
Public Act #87–1167
Effective January 1, 1993

Be It Enacted by the Legislature of the State of Illinois:

RITUALIZED ABUSE OF A CHILD—EXCLUSIONS—PENALTIES—
DEFINITION.

(a) A person is guilty of a felony when he commits any of the following acts with, upon, or in the presence of a child as part of a ceremony, rite, or similar observance.

    (1) actually or in simulation, tortures, mutilates or sacrifices any warm-blooded animal or human being;

    (2) forces ingestion, injection or other application of any narcotic drug, hallucinogen or anaesthetic for the purpose of dulling sensitivity, cognition, recollection of, or resistance to any criminal activity;

    (3) forces ingestion or external application of human or animal urine, feces, flesh, blood, bones, body secretions, nonprescribed drugs or chemical compounds;

    (4) involves the child in a mock, unauthorized or unlawful marriage ceremony with another person or representation of any force or deity, followed by sexual contact with the child;

(5) places a living child into a coffin or open grave containing a human corpse or remains;

(6) threatens death or serious harm to a child, his or her parents, family, pets, or friends which instills a well-founded fear in the child that the threat will be carried out; or

(7) unlawfully dissects, mutilates or incinerates a human corpse.

A *cult* is a group of people who share an obsessive devotion to a person or idea. The cults described in this book use violent tactics to recruit, indoctrinate, and keep members. Ritual abuse is defined as the emotionally, physically, and sexually abusive acts performed by violent cults. Most violent cults do not openly express their beliefs and practices, and they tend to live separately in noncommunal environments to avoid detection.

Some victims of ritual abuse are children abused outside the home by nonfamily members, in public settings such as day care. Other victims are children and teenagers who are forced by their parents to witness and participate in violent rituals. Adult ritual abuse victims often include these grown children who were forced from childhood to be a member of the group. Other adult and teenage victims are people who unknowingly joined social groups or organizations that slowly manipulated and blackmailed them into becoming permanent members of the group. All cases of ritual abuse, no matter what the age of the victim, involve intense physical and emotional trauma.

Violent cults may sacrifice humans and animals as part of religious rituals. They use torture to silence victims and other unwilling participants. Ritual abuse victims say they are degraded and humiliated and are often forced to torture, kill, and sexually violate other helpless victims. The purpose of the ritual abuse is usually indoctrination. The cults intend to destroy these victims' free will by undermining their sense of safety in the world and by forcing them to hurt others.

In the last ten years, a number of people have been convicted on sexual abuse charges in cases where the abused children had reported elements of ritual child abuse. These children described being raped by groups of adults who wore costumes or masks and said they were forced to witness religious-type rituals in which animals and humans were tortured or killed. In one case, the defense introduced in court photographs of the children being abused by the defendants.[1] In another case, the police found tunnels etched with crosses and pentacles along with stone altars and candles in a cemetery where abuse had been reported. The defendants in this case pleaded guilty to charges of incest, cruelty, and indecent assault.[2] Ritual abuse allegations have been made in England, the United States, and Canada.[3]

Many myths abound concerning the parents and children who report ritual abuse. Some people suggest that the tales of ritual abuse are "mass hysteria." They say the parents of these children who report ritual abuse are often overly zealous Christians on a "witch-hunt" to persecute satanists. These skeptics say the parents are fearful of satanism, and they use their knowledge of the Black Mass (a historically well-known, sexualized ritual in which animals and humans are sacrificed) to brainwash their children into saying they were abused by satanists.[4] In 1992 I conducted a study to separate fact from fiction in regard to the disclosures of children who report ritual abuse.[5] The study was conducted through Believe the Children, a national organization that provides support and educational sources for ritual abuse survivors and their families.

The first question in the study asked parents whether they were fearful of satanism prior to their child's disclosure of the ritual abuse. The results indicated that only two of the eleven parents were fearful of satanism. Eight of the parents reported they knew nothing about the elements of a Black Mass before their child first told them about the ritual abuse. The parents who are accused of being overly zealous Christians on a modern-day witch-hunt express frustration, as exemplified by one mother in the study.

Parents *don't want to believe* this would happen to their child. When my daughter said the janitor had touched her vagina, I suggested maybe it was her tummy instead. I didn't want to believe any of it. But I couldn't shut out what she was saying. The public needs to know that going through the disclosure process is excruciating for the child and the parents. There were occasions when I vomited after hearing disclosures, many nights I didn't sleep at all, and countless tears were shed. It would have been much easier not to believe it—she would have been forced to repress the trauma and would have had to deal with the overwhelming guilt I felt, the fear of retaliation, the outrage, and grief of having lost the relationship I thought I had with my child. She lost her innocence and her right to a normal childhood, and I lost my faith in the world and in our legal system.

She blamed me for sending her to the preschool where she was abused. I had to absorb her anger, pain—all her overwhelming feelings—without taking it personally. A hard thing to do when you want your child's love so much. We have repaired that bond that was frayed by the abuse, but there are scars that will never go away. Why would any parent want to put themselves—and their child—on such an emotional roller coaster? What have the children or parents gained from making ritual abuse allegations? We have been ridiculed, ostracized, and abandoned. I think of the old adage, "Kids lie to get out of trouble, not to get in trouble." Making allegations of ritual abuse gets you in *big* trouble! Why would anyone—child, parent, or survivor—lie about something so objectionable and unacceptable by most members of society?

The children not only describe seeing a human or animal killed, but having to participate in the killing. By disclosing they are incriminating themselves—getting themselves in trouble—at least, that is their perception of what will happen. They have no motive to do that unless they are telling the truth.

Another mother in the study said her six-year-old child never verbally disclosed the ritual abuse, but the behavior of her child made her speculate the child was abused in a systematic, violent fashion. She knew nothing about the Black Mass before her child started acting out the ritual abuse.

She began drawing pictures of witches, people with knives, pictures with the bones exposed in the throat area.

She also would get into trancelike states, and at one point
pulled a knife on her brother. On another occasion, she
had placed a butcher knife at her throat and was lovingly
caressing the blade of the knife. Two days later she pointed a
pair of scissors at her chest and asked where her heart was.
She consistently, for two-and-a-half years (from age four), has
bound and gagged just about every stuffed animal and Barbie
doll she owns. Her drawings also include bondage.

All eight of the children in this study who told their parents
about the ritual abuse—as opposed to only acting out the abuse—
were under the age of five. One grandmother in the study noted in
detail what her grandson, age three, and granddaughter, age two,
told her the first time they mentioned the ritual abuse.

To me, his grandmother, [the boy said,] "Mommy cut my
penis with her teeth. There was a lot of blood, here," he said,
indicating his lower abdomen. We had observed a couple of
months prior, a cut on his penis after a visit with his mother.
It had since healed. At that point it would never have
occurred to us that *she* would have done it. We assumed he
had accidentally injured himself. My granddaughter [said]:
"Sally [her mother] pooped on me."

The grandmother was asked in the questionnaire how she knew
the two children were telling the truth. She said,

The fear, the tone of voice, the clinging, the shame. Also,
I know them. I know the perpetrator. There was a sense of
intense gratitude from the children that I believed them.

After the children told her about the abuse, the grandmother
made a number of phone calls to find a therapist for them. Both
children are now in therapy, talking about their experiences. In the
same questionnaire, the children's therapist also noted her recollec-
tions of the children's first disclosures of abuse.

First disclosure was regarding Mom's abuse—Mom
touched chest, vagina, penis, pooped and peed all over me,
put me inside a pillow case, put us in a bathtub and covered
it so we couldn't get out, tied us up with ropes . . .

The therapist also noted why she believed the children.

There was a great deal of intensity of feeling and trauma communicated. Showed intense fear of retaliation, had flashbacks during sessions and would become physically and verbally abusive and violent. Would curl up in a fetal position and become mute. Consistency of report over time.

The therapist provided a list of behaviors exhibited by the two children that indicated ritual abuse.

Description and artwork delineating a group of individuals wearing different costumes with different cult "jobs." Fear of being killed by cult. Flashbacks. Sudden changes in behavior and voice when describing events. Sexual acting out during sessions. Violent outbursts—i.e., breaking mirrors. Fear of being confined. Intense separation anxiety. Obsession with confining, tying up self and others during play. Acting out the administration of drugs during their play. Setting up ritual scenes repeatedly in the sand tray. Artwork reflecting ritual acts, lots of blood. Appearing to have multiple personalities or fragments.

The grandmother reported the crimes to the police, but no charges were filed. At the end of the questionnaire, the grandmother described her frustration and rage about her inability to protect the two children from their mother.

It is open season on children under the age of four in this country. They're not "court-worthy." Public education is a *must*. Whenever *any* crime is committed that is of a satanic or occult/cult nature it should at least be public knowledge that the occult or a cult member was involved in the crime and that, if correct, it was ritualistic. If the media and law enforcement have to pussy-foot around the term "satanic" fine. But "ritualistic" or "cult-like," "cult-style," "occult overtones"? Why not? It would go a long way in educating the public. And if something was overtly done in the name of Satan or in an act of worship to Satan, if that was the intent of the perpetrator, whether or not it is the official doctrine of the church of Satan, it should be included in newspaper accounts, and all other media accounts of the crime. A crime is a crime is a crime!

The practice of ritual abuse is a difficult topic for many people to confront. The children are tortured and brainwashed in order to assure their loyalty to the group. The memories of ritual abuse survivors are often so graphic and perverse that some people question whether any of these stories could be true. Yet ritual abuse survivors experience overwhelming pain and trauma-related symptoms as they remember the ritual abuse: They experience violent flashbacks; their bodies feel the same sensations they felt at the time they were attacked. This is the same traumatic memory process experienced by other torture survivors and by war veterans who were traumatized on the battlefield. Ritual abuse is a real, systematic practice happening in our country today.

RITUAL ABUSE IN PRESCHOOLS

The main purpose of cults that ritually abuse children is to indoctrinate as many members as possible. The more people they are able to get involved in their group, the easier it is for them to justify what they are doing. Often cults will infiltrate schools, churches, daycare centers—anywhere they can go in order to recruit new members. The children who are abused in these settings are usually under the age of five and are unable to protect themselves from the manipulations of the cults. The cults appear to search for such victims because they are easier to brainwash.

In the last five years, two studies were conducted comparing the similarities of reports of ritual abuse in day-care centers. The theory behind the research is that children from different parts of the country report remarkable similarities in the details of the ritual abuse. Since the children have no contact with one another, it is suggested that the similar stories indicate a widely practiced sexualized ritual that involves animal or human sacrifices.

In 1987 Believe the Children conducted a study on multivictim, multiperpetrator child abuse in day-care settings.[6] Parents of victims and professionals working with victims of abuse were asked to complete a questionnaire detailing the reports of these abuses.

Ninety-four percent of the respondents noted that the child reported being sexually abused by a group of adults. Seventy-eight percent of the respondents noted the child was photographed nude during the abusive acts. Fifty-nine percent of the respondents said the child described being drugged during the abuse, and 58 percent reported the child said he or she was forced to watch the mutilation or killing of animals. Sixty-four percent of the respondents reported that the child said he or she was silenced by threats that the child's parents would be killed if the child ever told of the abuse. Some respondents stated the children described the use of robes (48 percent), candles (36 percent), and knives (36 percent) during the abuse. See Table 1.1 for a summary of these results.

A second study, conducted by therapist Pamela Hudson, noted the similarities in the finite details of ritual abuse allegations from nine day-care centers in five different states.[7] In these cases, either the police or the parents of the children defined the abuse as ritual child abuse. No standard definition of ritual abuse exists for parents and professionals.

Believe the Children provided Hudson with the names of parents from each of the nine day-care centers in which ritual abuse had been reported. The parents in each of these cases initially contacted Believe the Children to receive information and referrals that would enable them to help their children recover from the trauma of this abuse. The parents were interviewed over the phone regarding the details of what occurred during the ritual abuse.

In all these day-care centers (100 percent), medical examiners found evidence during examination commensurate with sexual abuse. All the reports (100 percent) said that the children had been filmed or photographed while the abuse took place. Parents also stated that the children described having been injected with drugs or poked with needles (100 percent). In nearly all of the reports (88 percent) from these day-care centers, children said they had been forced to watch animals being tortured and killed. The parents (100 percent) stated the abusers had threatened to kill the children's parents, siblings, or pets if the children ever told. In all the preschools (100 percent), parents noted that the children had been sexually abused by individuals wearing masks, robes, and carrying candles. Parents reported that the children (100 percent) said they had been taken away from the center for further abuse in churches,

graveyards, or other day-care centers. See Table 1.1 for a summary of
these results.

The first study mentioned above compared the differences in
individual ritual abuse cases from across the country. The results
indicated remarkable consistency in the details of the ritual abuse.
The second study examined the abuse allegations in day-care centers in which ritual abuse was reported. The results illustrated that
in spite of the vague definition of ritual abuse available to parents
and law enforcement professionals, there are remarkably detailed
similarities in the types of abuse perpetrated against these children
in different environments. Table 1.1 compares similarities in the
results of the two studies.

One limitation of the studies that some people suggest is that
these children and adults were led—by parents, children's agencies,
or prosecutors—to report abuse that never occurred. It is speculated that the parents, agencies, or prosecutors were aware of the
elements of a Black Mass, and they brainwashed the children into
believing things had happened that never actually occurred.

Some people suggest that parents of children who report ritual
abuse are paranoid or delusional fundamentalist Christians who
see satanists under every tree. However, as noted in the study I

**Table 1.1   Comparison of Allegations of Ritual
Child Abuse**

	Individual Cases (Children)	Day-Care Centers
Sexually abused by adults	94%	100%
Photographed nude	78%	100%
Drugged during abuse	59%	100%
Mutilation or killing of animals/humans	58%	88%
Silenced by threats of harm to family	64%	100%
Use of robes, candles, and/or knives during ritual	48%	100%

conducted through Believe the Children, none of the parents who participated in that study identified themselves as fundamentalist Christians. Many of the parents said they did not attend church on a regular basis. Again, almost none of the parents were fearful of satanism prior to their child's disclosure of the ritual abuse.

It is not in the best interests of children's agencies and prosecutors to brainwash children to report abuse that never occurred. Children's agencies are there to protect children from violence. They have no personal investment in brainwashing children for their own gain. In fact, it is more difficult to protect children who report ritual abuse.

Prosecutors base their success on how many cases they are able to win. Brainwashing children to make ritual abuse allegations diminishes the prosecutor's chances of winning the case, and hence it is counterproductive. It is extremely difficult to win a ritual abuse case. In fact, a number of parents of ritually abused children report that law enforcement professionals attempt to downplay the ritual elements the child describes. Prosecutors realize that if they bring the case to trial as "ritual abuse," they will have a difficult time convincing the jury of the credibility of the child's testimony. By ignoring the ritual abuse allegations, the prosecutors are able to maintain a higher conviction ratio, thus furthering their own careers.

ADULT SURVIVORS OF CHILDHOOD
RITUAL ABUSE

The reports of abuse by these children are echoed in another study, which examines the similarities in abuse histories reported by adult survivors of childhood ritual abuse. Lynda Driscoll and Cheryl Wright, Ph.D., conducted a study through the University of Utah in 1991 on the experiences of adult ritual abuse survivors.[8] The adult survivors of ritual abuse who volunteered for the study were in therapy for childhood trauma at the time they participated in the research. Thirty-seven adult survivors of childhood ritual abuse completed the questionnaire. Thirty-six of the survivors were female.

Like the children, 89 percent of the adult survivors said they had been molested by a group of adults, and 57 percent of the survivors said they had been photographed during the abuse. Seventy-eight percent of the survivors reported having been drugged during the abuse. Eighty-four percent of the survivors reported they had been forced to witness or participate in human sacrifice. Fifty-seven percent of the survivors reported having been told that their parents or relatives would be killed if they ever told anyone about the ritual abuse. The adult survivors noted that as children, they had been abused by a group of individuals wearing robes (95 percent) and masks (60 percent). Survivors reported having been abused in group members' homes (64 percent), wooded areas (64 percent), cemeteries (47 percent), churches (47 percent), and their own homes (43 percent). Table 1.2 presents the similarities between the adult survivors' memories of ritual abuse and the results of the two studies described earlier in this chapter on children's memories of ritual abuse.

Some people suggest that therapists who treat ritual abuse survivors brainwash their clients into believing they experienced things that never happened. Others say that survivors are delusional or merely seeking attention.[9] By labeling someone as "mentally ill"

Table 1.2 Comparison of Allegations of Child and Adult Survivors of Ritual Abuse

	Individual Cases (Children)	Day-Care Centers	Adults in Therapy
Sexually abused by adults	94%	100%	89%
Photographed nude	78%	100%	57%
Drugged during abuse	59%	100%	78%
Mutilation or killing of animals/humans	58%	88%	84%
Silenced by threats of harm to family	64%	100%	57%
Use of robes, candles, and/or knives during ritual	48%	100%	95%

or downright crazy, one can immediately discount everything the person says. This tactic is successful in shaming most ritual abuse survivors into silence.

It is not realistic to suggest that people would identify themselves as ritual abuse survivors merely because they are bored or want attention. Women and men who identify themselves as ritual abuse survivors find themselves blamed for the abuse. They are not believed by therapists, police officers, clergy, or friends, even though many ritual abuse survivors are respected members of our communities. They remember the abuse through a traumatic memory process that includes all the emotional feelings and physical sensations they experienced during the abuse.

Another common tactic used to discredit survivors and their advocates is to compare current talk of ritual abuse to the witch-hunts of the seventeenth century. This argument is an emotional plea that taps into society's justifiable guilt about the injustices committed during the Inquisition and the Salem witch-hunts, when innocent victims were publicly humiliated and slaughtered in the name of the Christian God. The witch-hunts were one of the most inhumane and unjust times in all of history. Consequently, it is important to understand the very clear distinctions between the witch-hunts of the past and what we hear about ritual abuse today.

First, the witch-hunts were primed by the publication of a single book, *Malleus Maleficarum* (*The Hammer of the Witches*), in 1486. In this book, the authors, both Christian monks, delineated the characteristics of a "witch." One example of "normal female witch behavior" in the book describes how a female witch takes the spirit away from the male sex organ, which results in male impotence or castration. Punishments of female witches included bathing in boiling water, crushing by heavy weights, tearing the flesh from the breasts with searing-hot pincers, and torture of the female sex organs. These punishments are similar to the graphic stories told of ritual abuse today. However, during the witch-hunts, the punishments were committed in order to restore the Christian God's blessing onto the community.

In Salem, Massachusetts, in the 1690s, five types of evidence were accepted as proof of witch behavior. One type of evidence included forcing the accused witch to say the Lord's Prayer in public. Since witches were assumed to say the Lord's Prayer backwards, if the accused made a slip, this proved she was indeed a witch. The second type of evidence was the witness of people who blamed their own misfortunes on the magical powers of the accused. The third type of evidence was the presence of "devil's marks" on the accused—warts, moles, scars, or other bodily imperfections. The fourth was a confession of guilt—often obtained under torture. The final type of evidence was reports from people who said they had seen floating ghostlike forms of the accused.

In those days, people accused of witchcraft—most of them innocent women—were not given a trial. In Europe even children accused of witchcraft were condemned to horrifying punishments. When the community decided a person was a witch, the punishment was torture or execution. Sometimes the community imprisoned the person in a stockade for onlookers to taunt and harass.[10]

Clearly, what we have today is not a witch-hunt. Law enforcement and overly zealous Christians have not been given a license to go after anyone they want. No criteria exists to help therapists, parents, children's agencies, and prosecutors determine who is a "satanist." In fact, the people accused of ritual abuse today have few common characteristics. They are not card-carrying members of the Church of Satan; they are a variety of people accused of similar acts. What we have today is a cross section of people from around the world who are talking about a common ritual context in which children are being abused.

Each time we discount the memories of ritual abuse survivors, we make a very clear choice. If there is a chance these children and adults are telling the truth, and children are being horribly abused in rituals today, then we have a responsibility to these victims to take seriously those people who are talking about it. As a society, we have the responsibility to protect the victims, both the children and adults, from further harm.

THE SURVIVORS

Much of the information in this book is based on a sociological study of ritual abuse. The survivors who volunteered for this study were adult survivors of childhood ritual abuse. They completed a detailed questionnaire, which is presented in Appendix A. All survivors were required to be in therapy at the time they completed the questionnaire, to assure that survivors had support while they confronted such a painful topic.

Ritual abuse survivors are not social outcasts. They are not freaks. Many people may be surprised to find out that most survivors of ritual abuse are functioning members of our society. During the past ten years, a number of organizations have formed to provide education and support for people whose lives have been affected by ritual child abuse. Each of the following organizations and newsletters placed announcements asking for volunteers to complete a questionnaire on ritual abuse:

Believe the Children is a national organization that provides support and education for families of children who have been ritually abused in day-care settings.

The Ritual Abuse Awareness Network is a national organization that provides educational material on ritual abuse.

Healing Hearts of Berkeley, California, provides workshops and educational materials for therapists and survivors.

Voices in Action is an organization for survivors of incest and also provides information on ritual abuse.

Survivorship and *Many Voices* are newsletters to which many ritual abuse survivors subscribe.

Gender, Race, and Occupation

Fifty women and two men responded to the announcements and completed the questionnaire. Fifty of the survivors in this study are white, one is Asian, and one is African-American. Nearly all of the survivors were employed at the time they completed the questionnaire. The following is a list of their occupations:

- four college students
- four counselors
- four disability recipients
- four homemakers

- three college professors
- three teachers
- three artists
- two administrative assistants
- two nurses
- two office managers
- one data coordinator
- one human services employee
- one lead systems analyst
- one medical technician
- one management analyst
- one chauffeur
- one botanist/writer
- one dental assistant
- one carpenter
- one office worker
- one engineer
- one laboratory technician
- one feminist health-care administrator
- one director of religious education
- one owner and director of a learning center

Six survivors chose not to answer this question. One survivor said, "I'm a person trying to live. That is my occupation." The survivors who volunteered for this study are in many ways like most members of society. They go to work, have relationships, and struggle with the same day-to-day problems we all experience.

Geographical Location

Most of the survivors who volunteered for this study lived in California (40 percent), possibly because more resources are available for ritual abuse survivors in California than in any other state. Significantly more therapists in California are trained to treat survivors of ritual abuse, and support groups exist to help them. A number of rape crisis teams and sexual assault centers in the state are trained on ritual abuse. Survivors of ritual abuse who live in California are probably more likely to search for help than survivors who live in other states, where resources for ritual abuse survivors are not readily available. Table 1.3 lists all the states where survivors in this study lived at the time they answered the questionnaire.

Socioeconomic Status

At the turn of the century, when child abuse was first acknowledged, it was described as "child mistreatment as a result of poverty." The state identified the children as the problem, not the parents who abused them. The children were sent to rehabilitation homes because it was believed that they posed a future threat to the larger society.[11] Today society is aware that child abuse is a problem in all socioeconomic classes.

This study shows that ritual abuse is not confined to a single social class (see Table 1.4). It is easier for most of us to imagine that people who were severely abused were raised in the lower class. It is difficult to imagine that the wealthy, powerful people in our communities—those people who often have control over our lives—could beat and molest their children. It is even more frightening to imagine that such people are members of cults.

Religious Upbringing

Many readers will also be surprised to learn that nearly all the survivors in this study reported having been raised in a family that practiced a mainstream religion (see Table 1.5). Many survivors in this study who were abused by their families stated that their parents were pillars of the religious community. This made it very confusing when the memories of the ritual abuse surfaced. One survivor noted in detail her religious upbringing:

> . . . our family was strictly religious . . . I can safely say
> that I did not miss church on Sunday more than five times

Table 1.3   States and Countries from Which Questionnaires Were Mailed

California	40%	Minnesota	2%
Washington	10%	Connecticut	2%
Colorado	8%	Montana	2%
Ohio	6%	Kentucky	2%
New York	4%	Indiana	2%
Louisiana	4%	Massachusetts	2%
Georgia	4%	Wisconsin	2%
Florida	2%	Canada	2%
Texas	2%	Japan	2%
Virginia	2%		

Table 1.4   Social Class in Which Survivors Were Raised

Upper class	4%	Working class	32%
Upper-middle class	30%	Lower class	4%
Middle class	30%		

Table 1.5   Religion in Which Survivors Were Formally Raised

Protestant	63%	Atheist	4%
Catholic	19%	Born-Again Christian	2%
None	6%	Other: Non-denominational Christian	2%
Jewish	4%		

during the entire time from when I was born till age eighteen. We had family prayers before every meal and family devotions many nights. The children were all baptized infants and "confirmed" into the church at age thirteen. My mother (one of the abusers) spoke to us numerous times about how important it was to her to have Christian faith, and how calling on the Lord in time of trouble is the only way to make it in life.

Aleister Crowley, a well-known British occultist living at the turn of the century, made a reference to a hidden church behind our traditional churches. In his book *The Confessions of Aleister Crowley,* he describes his search for "truth" through the occult. He stated that in his search, he continued to meet people who told him that "behind the exterior of the church is an interior church, the most hidden of all communities, a Secret Sanctuary which preserves all the mysteries of God and nature. It was formed after the fall of man. It is the hidden assembly of the Elect."

Intrigued by this hidden church, Crowley spent a number of years in search of this Secret Sanctuary. He was led by friends to a number of secret societies and fraternal orders that claimed to carry a secret knowledge about God.[12] In light of this theory about a "secret church within the church," it is not surprising that survivors in this study reported their parents were members of churches and religious organizations that are not satanic in nature.

Age of Survivors

The ages of people who responded to the questionnaire ranged from twenty-four to fifty-five at the time of this questionnaire; the average age was thirty-six (see Table 1.6). The small number of survivors in their twenties who volunteered for this study may indicate that remembering such extreme trauma is difficult to do at a young age. Most survivors of ritual abuse are unable to remember the abuse until they are financially stable. During their twenties, children sometimes still depend on their parents for financial assistance. Dependence on the family of origin is often much greater before children establish a family of their own. It is difficult

Table 1.6 Ages of the Survivors Who Participated
in This Study

20 to 25	4%	41 to 45	19%
26 to 30	13%	46 to 50	12%
31 to 35	15%	51 to 55	8%
36 to 40	29%	56 to 60	0%

to confront the memories of abuse until the survivor has achieved
a certain amount of distance from the abusers.

It is also likely that mid-life crisis drives both survivors and
nonsurvivors to confront their pasts. At this time, people start to
question what they are doing with their lives. They ask themselves,
"What is really important? Have I found what I am looking for?"
They begin to reflect on childhood issues, such as abuse, that they
have forgotten or tried to ignore.

People in their fifties and sixties are probably more likely simply to accept the things they don't believe they can change. Their
time of raising a family is over. What's done is done. At this point,
it seems easier to let the past be the past and to accept that they may
have lost many things they believe can never be regained.

Limitations of the Study

The results of this study do not represent the experience of all ritual
abuse survivors. A number of limitations to this study make it impossible to generalize about survivors. First, the survivors who
completed this questionnaire are only *the survivors who have remembered*. Ninety-seven percent of the survivors in this study said
that at some point during their lives, they were amnesic of their
ritual abuse experience. This means an unknown number of survivors are presently unaware of their ritual abuse history. What we
know about these people is what we can infer from information
provided by remembering survivors. These remembering women
and men often can describe what their lives were like before they

remembered the ritual abuse. However, it is likely that remembering survivors have more symptoms of trauma than nonremembering ritual abuse survivors. It is probable that the very symptoms of trauma that drove them into therapy also enabled them to remember the abuse. Appendix B lists a number of symptoms survivors had before they remembered the ritual abuse, and which might have suggested they were ritually abused as children.

Second, the requirement for survivors to be in therapy limits the results of this study. Survivors who are unable to find satisfactory therapy because of financial limitations are inadequately represented. Survivors who have looked to clergy or other means for their emotional support are also not represented here. Finally, as this book will illustrate, many survivors have grown weary of being revictimized by mental health professionals and have given up therapy altogether.

CHILD ABUSE: A HISTORICAL PERSPECTIVE

Why do we hear so much about child abuse today? One reason is that disciplinary techniques considered acceptable less than fifty years ago are now legally defined as child abuse. For example, earlier in this century, schoolchildren were regularly paddled and whacked with rulers or boards on their knuckles and bottoms as a means of discipline for minor infractions. Today physical child abuse is legally defined as any assault against a child that leaves a physical injury—a mark. Until less than thirty years ago, there were no laws to protect children from violence.

Not only were children beaten at school, but the church in the early 1800s also made a number of public statements advocating corporal punishment. The church declared that before the age of five, parents must literally beat the spirit out of the child or else the child would become "spoiled." This church suggestion followed the old saying, "Spare the rod, spoil the child." Physical punishments that left marks on children, acts that are now illegal, were practiced in schools as "discipline" and encouraged by religious authorities.

The cyclical nature of violence is a clear consequence of child abuse. Sometimes those who were abused as children can feel a strong, almost uncontrollable impulse to reenact the abuse on their own children. Unless these parents realize that they are stuck in a cycle that must be broken—unless they find some way to control themselves from acting on impulse—they often act on their feelings and hurt the child. The implications are clear: If hitting a child was once an acceptable form of discipline, and the desire to harm a child is passed from generation to generation, then it is likely that many people abuse children today without defining it as such. This cycle of violence against children—and the fact that violence against children was socially acceptable in this country less than fifty years ago—keeps many people from honestly confronting the problem. Our inability to protect children from violence has allowed cults that practice ritual abuse to flourish.

Dissociation

It is difficult to imagine that people who have experienced ritual abuse could be alive and functioning in our society today. It is even more difficult to imagine that survivors go to college and teach at our local universities. Where do all their feelings go? How could someone be exposed to so much pain and not feel it today? The answer is a process referred to as *dissociation*—escaping an intolerable situation by detaching oneself mentally and emotionally. When children are exposed to extreme pain, their minds desperately try to stop it. Sometimes the mind is successful, sometimes it is not. When it is successful, children are able to completely forget about the abuse and the pain it caused.

Traumatic amnesia is common among ritual abuse survivors. When children are severely abused by people who have control over their every movement (such as parents or guardians), the pain from the abuse becomes too much for them to allow in their daily experiences. For example, it would be too overwhelming for a child to go to school each day and remember being ritually abused in a cult the night before, so the child learns never to think about the abuse except for when it is happening. A child who is ritually abused over time develops a mental place that remembers only the abuse, and another place that attempts to live a "normal" life at school and with people outside the cult. Unfortunately, when the child learns to forget about the abuse, he or she is at the complete mercy of the abusers. What saved the child's sanity and life, the amnesia, is often the most powerful force that keeps the child from leaving the group later. By cutting off from the reality of the abuse in the cults, the child is able to stop the pain. But by forgetting, the child is also unable to make choices that would prevent further victimization as an adult.

Amnesia of severe trauma is a widely acknowledged consequence of war. War veterans are often amnesic about the most traumatic events they faced on the battlefield. The traumatic memories veterans experience are usually in the form of flashbacks. Their minds actually believe they are back at that very same moment when the trauma occurred. During the flashbacks, the veterans experience all the physical sensations and emotions they experienced at the time of the trauma.

Within the last decade, professionals have noted these same traumatic symptoms in people who were severely abused as children. Often the symptoms of trauma from child abuse have been falsely identified by professionals—even by the child abuse survivors themselves—as hypersensitivity, hypochondria, or even schizophrenia. The physical and sexual attack on a child by a parent or guardian is easily compared to the trauma soldiers face during a battle. However, in many ways the violent attack on a child by a parent may result in greater pain.

First, children are utterly dependent on adults to meet all their physical needs. The enemy, the adult abuser, is also the same person who is keeping the children alive by feeding them and clothing them. In war, soldiers are usually not ambivalent toward the enemy. They don't have to live with the enemy or smile at them every day. Second, children's minds cognitively have a difficult time separating truth from lies. They are unable to protect themselves from the manipulation abusers use to control them. The adult mind can rationalize, think for itself, and sort through lies. Third, children abused by their parents often know of no other world than the violent, cold world in which they are being raised. The minds of adult soldiers are already aware of their own identity and past prior to the trauma they face during battle. Finally, children are emotionally the most vulnerable creatures on the earth. They are affected by every verbal or physical blow, whereas most adults have already learned to mentally protect themselves from attack.

The problem of ritual abuse is complex, as this book will make clear. I do not want to shelter anyone from the truth, and as a result this book may be very painful to read. At times the survivor's predicament may appear hopeless, but this is not the case. In awareness, there is hope. In education and in support, there is hope. I would like this book to serve as a validation and support resource for all of us who have been through the ordeal of ritual abuse and to provide comfort and understanding for our hidden places of silenced pain.

NOTES

1. "Sensational Cases Across the Country," "Cases from the Bay Area and the West," *San Francisco Examiner* (September 28, 1989): A9.

2. "Vortex of Evil," *New Statesman and Society* (October 5, 1990).

3. Beth Marlin, "The Cannibal Case," *Canadian Lawyer* (October 1987): 24–27.

4. Arthur Lyons, *Satan Wants You* (New York: The Mysterious Press, 1988), 146 and 153.

5. Margaret Smith, *Children Abused in Violent Rituals: Fact or Fiction?* (Woodland, CA: Reaching Out, 1992), 3–16.

6. Believe the Children, "Multi-victim Multi-perpetrator Ritualized Abuse Survey," preliminary results, June 1987. Unpublished manuscript.

7. Pamela Hudson, *Ritual Child Abuse: Discovery, Diagnosis and Treatment* (Saratoga, CA: R & E Publishers, 1991), 26–28.

8. Lynda N. Driscoll and Cheryl Wright, Ph.D., "Survivors of Childhood Ritual Abuse: Multi-generational Satanic Cult Involvement," *Treating Abuse Today* 1, no. 4 (September/October 1991): 5–13.

9. J. Johnson and S. Padilla, "Satanism: Skeptics Abound," *Los Angeles Times* (April 23, 1991): A20.

10. Steven Pfohl, *Images of Deviance and Social Control* (New York: McGraw-Hill, 1985), 24–40.

11. Steven Pfohl, "The Discovery of Child Abuse," *Social Problems* 24:3 (February 1977): 310–23.

12. Aleister Crowley, *The Confessions of Aleister Crowley,* edited by John Symonds and Kenneth Grant (London: Arkana, 1979), 16.

Chapter 2

Understanding Multiple Personality Disorder

To me, having multiple personalities does not feel like I have lots of people living inside my body. Rather I find myself thinking and talking to myself in different tones and dialects.

Some of the voices that talk in my mind sound like children. When I allow them to talk to other people they don't talk like children to impress anyone or to be dramatic; I have to talk like that sometimes in order to express what I need to say. I can't say it from my adult voice—the same ideas and feelings wouldn't come out. When I go outside and listen to real children, I notice my kid voices sound just like them. I make the same grammatical slips. I use the same tones with the same feelings. And I don't plan to make the voices sound that way. That's just how the words come out of my mouth!

Then there are the deep, raspy, intent voices that say the meanest things you could imagine. When they talk, I feel hard inside. I feel cold and calculating. People are usually horrified by what these voices say, but I am not afraid or ashamed of them. I like it when they talk because they express feelings that I have trouble articulating. When they talk, I agree with them completely, but I have other perspectives as well. I also know what it feels like to be the little kid voice that felt hurt and vulnerable.

The different voices really start rapping when I talk about the ritual abuse. I usually talk like a normal person—one tone, adult voice—but if I start to talk about cult things, the other voices come in and do all the talking for me. I don't think about what they are saying. It just flows out of my mouth. Sometimes I evaluate the voices to see if what they are saying is true. I compare it with the past I remember. It always seems to fit. The voices rarely contradict themselves. For example, once a personality recounted a certain abuse experience, and I ended up forgetting the memory after a few days. Two years later, a new personality began to talk about the same memory I had repressed. Both personalities recalled the same details. I verified this by reading my old journals. The two personalities had different feelings and perspectives about what happened, but the situation they described was the same.

It's easy to hide the multiplicity. All I have to do is believe it's not there and never talk about cult things. Before I knew about the ritual abuse, I probably looked moody. My tone of voice would never change enough for people to notice the switches. I never intentionally hid the voices from other people. The traumatized voices just never spoke because they knew it wasn't socially acceptable to talk like a baby or a homicidal killer. They had to be silent if I wanted other people to like me.

Multiple Personality Disorder—MPD—is not a game. It's not "acting" to impress anyone. Trust me, survivors do not receive positive attention for being a multiple. Anyone who fakes it would be setting themselves up for a lot of rejection. Letting my personalities speak is the only way I can tap into my own personal truth. If I don't let these guys talk—and if I don't listen to what they are saying—then my life is hollow and empty. I would be living my life for society, sacrificing my own truth, so that people wouldn't look down on me or label me as a freak or a sucker who has been manipulated into believing I have a disorder that is as rare as the bubonic plague.

When my personalities finally talk, it feels so natural. After letting one of them talk, I feel more connected to myself, more real, more true to who I really am. Some of me feels hokey calling them personalities. They really are just me. All the little voices that I talk about as if they were other people are me. Nothing is wrong with them; nothing is wrong with me. Maybe someday I will be able to express all my feelings in one voice—maybe I will always have to use different voices to say what I mean—but I don't think people should try to silence those voices simply because they don't believe in MPD.

Most people, multiples and nonmultiples alike, have experienced times when it seems we are required not to feel. Each time we attempt to meet a demand of the environment that contradicts our emotional experience, we have to cut ourselves off from our conflicting emotions. We are taught to conform to family and societal rules despite how we might feel about the rules. We are told as children not to punch our little brother when we feel anger. We are told to act socially appropriate. If we don't conform, we are punished—a little spanking or maybe a slap—or worse, some of us are taught that we are somehow "bad" or "unlovable." The power of shaming children—making them believe that they do not belong or that they are defective inside—is the most powerful tool people use to force children to conform.

Later in life, our feelings are often controlled by the authority of the person who gives us money; be it an employer or a spouse. For example, a woman who is financially dependent on her husband may sometimes feel that she must hide her angry or resentful feelings. She may be afraid that if she expressed what she was really feeling, he would leave her and she would have no way to support herself and her children.

In the workplace, our feelings are once again controlled by our need for financial security. At home, most of us are able to express some of what we feel inside. We fight with our spouse and express our frustration to our children in ways that would never be acceptable on the job. At work, when the boss makes us angry, we are supposed to bite our tongues. We learn to hold in the feelings in order to maintain a professional atmosphere. If we have an emotional blowup, we risk losing our jobs.

As a result of holding in all these unacceptable feelings, many of us feel tied up in knots. We end up being uncertain about what we feel. Everyone tells us what we ought to think and feel, and eventually we are unable to separate what we truly feel from what someone told us. When we experience feelings that are not acceptable, we use techniques to help us keep them under control. Some people smoke or drink. Others eat a gallon of ice cream. Still others search for the perfect love that will make all the injustices seem bearable. All of these numbing techniques help to soothe the discomfort of

overwhelming emotions. We are able to soothe the painful feelings
that others seem to seldom acknowledge or understand. What we
are unable to do is to change what initially caused the pain.

Most of us also learn not to feel physical pain. As children, we
cried and cried when we scraped our knees. As adults, we drag ourselves to work with an excruciating cold without even shedding a
tear. When we are immersed in our work, we probably feel significantly better. But when we get home, we once again feel the aches
that we didn't feel at work. When we are alone—when we are not
distracted—is when we are most aware of our physical or emotional
pain.

Dissociation is the psychological term for this process of dis-
tancing ourselves from physical and emotional discomfort. The
term is primarily used to describe the mind's reaction to trauma.
For example, people who are raped dissociate in order to survive
the experience. Sexual attacks and physical torture are some of the
most devastating forms of violence committed against the body.
Often people who are sexually attacked or tortured become so overwhelmed with fear, nausea, and pain that they completely block out
details of the experience. Some people who are raped report floating above their bodies and watching the rape happen. Mystics and
parapsychologists refer to this as an out-of-body experience or a
soul in exile—the spirit is so unsafe in the body that it leaves.

Children who are sexually attacked are very likely to experience traumatic dissociation. Children are at the mercy of adults for
their very survival, so they can't allow themselves to feel the overwhelming helplessness and pain that is a result of the abuse. They
are unable to physically escape, but they often escape within their
minds. The process of traumatic dissociation that abused children
experience is probably less a conscious decision than a biological
response to relieve pain.

When traumatic dissociation occurs, often the mind spins from
the pain and confusion. Soon there is no solid ground on which the
mind can operate. The dizziness and sickness are too great. Sud-
denly, all the feelings are gone. Nothing is left but a numb emptiness. During ritual abuse, children can be so overwhelmed with
their emotions that they snap and are unable to remember who

they are or how they got there. The feelings disappear, leaving a mental blank spot—no words, no thoughts. A child in this condition will believe anything he or she is told.

During ritual abuse, the abusers continually bring children to this state of confusion and then tell them lies. For example, the abusers say the children really want to be hurt. They tell the children they are bad and that they belong with bad people. They tell the children that they are dirty and evil inside and that everyone sees the dirtiness. They try to make the children feel isolated from other people. They brainwash the children in order to force them to commit acts of violence. After the children are forced to commit violent acts, the abusers cite it as proof. "See, you are one of us," they say. Manipulating the children to believe they had a choice when they did not is a common brainwashing tactic used by cults that ritually abuse children.

While dissociating, often the children can't think. Their minds are unable to argue or disagree with the abusers. If the abuse continues over a long period, the children will eventually develop coping mechanisms to deal with the situation. Other voices will develop in their minds that identify themselves as not their own. For example, a young boy being ritually abused may find a voice that comforts him. The voice may emerge when he is in the "blank spot" to tell him the abusers are lying. The voice may say he is really a good, lovable little boy. He may also find a voice inside that regurgitates all the mean things the abusers say to him. By bringing this voice inside, the child has control over it. The world outside is dangerous and out of the child's control. The internal world is the only world that can exist in these moments of lost confusion. The voices that emerge while the child is traumatized never disappear. The voices are always there—even after the trauma has ceased, and whether they are listened to or not.

Children may hear a number of voices that help them to minimize the pain. Nonmultiples experience something similar when they remind themselves to do something they don't want to do. For example, a nonmultiple may wake up feeling bad and not want to go to work. A thought reminds him that if he doesn't go, there will be no food on the table next week. The abused child's voices are more powerful than these mild messages all people experience. Voices of multiple personalities are more developed in order to relieve the chronic pain from the abuse.

A child who is being abused desperately searches for a voice inside to soothe the pain. When the voices start to develop, more and more "personalities" may be born. What actually develops as a full-blown personality depends on how often the abuse occurs and on other environmental influences. If the ritual abuse happened only once or twice, the voices may become nothing more than parts of a memory. If the abuse was prolonged, the voices may take on a life of their own.

Take, for instance, a boy who heard voices in his mind as the abuse occurred. Later, if the situation demands it, the voices might "become" the child. For example, ritual abusers often tell children to betray the things they love. They set up situations in which the children are given a choice. The abusers say, "Either hurt your loved one, or we will hurt both of you." When the children do not comply with the demands of the cult, they and the other intended victim are both tortured. The young boy, when confronted with this predicament, would actually minimize his pain and his loved one's pain if he simply complied with the abusers the first time he was asked. Despite the logic behind his actions, however, hurting his loved one is still an extremely painful act. The abusive voice in the boy's mind is able to emerge and become the child while he commits the act of violence. In order to minimize the pain, the boy does not identify the actions the "voice" committed as his own. The voice has become another personality. It is easier for the child to forget what the voice had to do. Remembering would cause horrible feelings. The child learns to forget what happened when the voice "became" him. The amount of time that he cannot account for in his own memory is referred to in psychological terms as "lost time."

The personalities who develop during the abuse do not disappear once the original trauma ceases. They reemerge later in life if they are exposed to a situation reminiscent of the original abuse. For example, a survivor engaged in a fiery debate with her husband about rape may start to feel extremely helpless and panicked. She quickly becomes silent because she knows that she will start crying hysterically if she continues with the conversation. A survivor facing the decision to put a pet to sleep may also feel panicked. He may feel like he is responsible for the death. He starts to feel desperate and guilt-ridden. A personality who had to hurt the things he loved is triggered by this situation. A survivor breaking up with a lover may feel extremely desperate because the breakup reminds her of the abandonment she felt in childhood from her abusers and from the people who did not protect her. She perceives the breakup as "proof" that she will never be loved and protected. All of these seemingly irrational thoughts and feelings are other personalities reemerging as they are reminded of the original trauma. Survivors who can stop these personalities before they take control will not "lose time."

Children who are raised in cults continually require various personalities to emerge to meet the commands of the abusers. Most cults deliberately train these alter personalities to emerge only when they are triggered with specific cues. For example, survivors often note that they were told certain words or shown certain images while under torture, which the cult later uses to cause them to switch personalities. Once they are shown the trigger and switch personalities, the cult is able to control their behavior. For most ritual abuse survivors, alter personalities aware of the cult's activities emerge *only* during the ritual abuse. Some survivors may even be unaware of their own current cult involvement. Their alter personalities are continually at the mercy of the abusers. Cults program these personalities never to emerge in the survivors' daily lives. This keeps survivors from ever telling other people about the abuse. In these cases, survivors may never "lose time" in their non-cult lives.

PERSONALITIES BORN INSIDE THE CULT

Alter personalities develop to relieve the contradictory feelings ritual abuse survivors experience. Children can't love or find safety with their parents if they know they are taken to rituals and tortured, so the personality goes to the ritual for them. Each personality holds a piece of the child's experience. Each develops his or her own life, with different ways of speaking and dressing. The personalities are all in place to protect one another from the painful reality that they all are forced to experience. Survivors who have developed these separate voices and realities can distance themselves from the overwhelming feelings they cannot express in the moment.

In general, three different types of personalities seem to develop to cope with a long-term ritual abuse. The first type is born in the trauma of the ritual abuse. The second type develops over time to meet the demands of the day-to-day noncult experience. The final type emerges in the child's mind to facilitate the process of keeping the cult and noncult experiences separate.

We're going to look at different types of personalities that develop in each of these three contexts, but this information must be interpreted with caution. First, this is not an exhaustive list of personalities experienced by every victim. Most survivors develop unique names for their personalities. Also, there may be more types of personalities in a particular individual survivor's multiple "system" than the ones presented here. Survivors develop personalities to meet the demands of their unique abuse situation. Every multiple system is different.

Second, because personalities born in the cults are continually required to fragment their realities, a personality born to cope with a certain aspect of the trauma may also fragment. This first personality may also become a "multiple." For example, a personality born to kill things may be exposed to increasingly painful situations that he, she, or it cannot cope with alone. The personality may first be asked to kill an animal, then a pet, then another human child. Each time the personality has to commit a more painful act, a new personality may need to be born. If this is the case, the survivor develops subsystems of personalities within a single type of personality.

Third, the ages of personalities vary depending on the survivor's individual abuse experience. Although the age of the personality usually depends on when the personality was initially traumatized, there are no set rules. Some of the personalities are children. If the personality was traumatized into silence at a young age, the personality could remain that age until he or she reemerges later in the survivor's life. Other personalities born at a young age grow up as the child grows up; these personalities were never silenced. For example, a personality might have been born when the child was three, but today the personality has grown to become a thirty-six-year-old high priestess. This personality may talk in an adult voice as well as a child voice.

Finally, the personalities are not discrete. They are not real people living inside survivors; they are different ways that one individual perceives and relates to the world. Sometimes personalities might appear to be different enough to be separate people, but each personality is expressing a piece of a single individual's experience. They are all altered states of a single traumatized individual.

Personalities who are finally allowed to talk to each other and hear each other engage in a process called *communication*. By communicating their ideas, feelings, and thoughts, the personalities are finally able to meet each other and find common ground. As the personalities learn about one another, the boundaries between them begin to blur. They may no longer use separate names to address each other because this may make them feel too separate. They may begin to refer to themselves as "parts" of the same person. They may also like to use their names up until the point when they integrate. Using their names ensures that everyone is recognized and heard. Over time, the personalities learn to express themselves in an integrated voice that expresses the needs and desires of all personalities. We will discuss the process of communication and integration in greater detail after we look at the different types of personalities.

I'm Dying. Oh, God. Somebody Help Me!

"Dizzy, dizzy, dizzy. Spinning, falling. Oh, God, help! Someone please help!"

Desperation, pain, and panic are the original voices of the child. This is all the fear and all the pain that the child felt in the moment of abuse. These are the feelings that became too overwhelming for the ritual abuse survivor to experience. When the child felt this pain, nobody came to help. Nobody listened. Even as adults, survivors may feel as if they are not heard.

The fact is that many people do not believe ritual abuse survivors. People are more concerned with evidence or proof of abuse than with the feelings of the victims. Many people think survivors are crazy, others blame survivors for their own pain. There is a great deal of revictimization of ritual abuse survivors. The sad truth is that survivors today must be cautious about opening up the old wound.

However, if survivors persistently look for help—while taking care of themselves by not allowing themselves to be revictimized— they will eventually find people willing to listen to their truth without trying to make them feel ashamed. The process of reaching back to the original desperation and pain is not something that should be taken lightly. The process is extremely painful, and in many ways it can also be dangerous. The following chapters will describe these points in further detail. For now, it is important to note that those who face the pain are deeply rewarded for all their efforts. In the end, the personalities feel deep relief from not having to pretend they are something they are not. Everyone gets their freedom.

This Is Not Happening

"Me just fine. This no is happening. Me Daddy love me. He no would ever hurt me."

A child's first reaction to the abuse is to deny what is happening: "Daddy would never do this to me. Daddy loves me. This isn't happening." As the pain becomes more intense, these thoughts might sound like a voice speaking in a tunnel. The voice may start to echo in the child's mind and not even sound like his voice anymore. The child stops hearing the thoughts as his own. The thoughts become like someone else's voice living inside his head.

Where Am I? Who Am I?

"I can't see you. I can't feel you. Oh, God, I can't touch you!"

During severe physical trauma, there is a point where the mind and the body split. The mind forgets all the things it knew prior to the trauma. You can't think. Your vision is blurred, if not completely erased. Physical sensations also cease. This is one of the most frightening things anyone can experience. It feels as if you are dying. For multiples, a death does in fact occur: One personality dies, while another is born.

The sensation in the moment is that everything in the world has been sucked up into a black hole of nothingness. It is the end. At that point, a personality—a very real part of the survivor—dies, never to be heard from again. Fortunately, the death of a personality is not a permanent physical reality, but the emotional death of a part of the survivor. Life flows back into the dead personalities as other personalities realize their own personal truth. As the live personalities express their feelings to someone who really cares about them, the dead personalities are regenerated. They find their voice once again. The survivor once again finds his or her personal truth.

Physical Sensation

"All I can feel is a needle in the arm. They're sliding it in. Now I think it is something in the butt. I can feel it, but I can't see anything."

As the mind separates from the body, the physical sensations still remain. There is no mind to describe the sensations. The victim's body becomes "the body," not "my body." The survivor's mind cannot own the pain that the body has to endure.

The separation of mind and body is absolutely essential for a ritual abuse survivor. The body is screaming, "Stop, stop, stop!" but there is no physical way to stop what is happening. By separating the mind into a hundred different voices, and by allowing the body merely to feel unidentified physical sensations, the child is able to stop the pain.

After the trauma has ceased, the physical sensations will recur in the body as *body memories*. Specific incidents will remind the body of the original trauma, and the body will feel the pain as intensely as if it is being traumatized at that moment. For example, a survivor may experience an unidentifiable pain in her arm, as if someone is sticking a needle in it. Or she might feel a sharp pain in her anus. When these body memories surface, the mind remains separate from the body. The sensations in the body feel very distant from any thoughts about the pain.

Body memories are the grounding force for all the confusion in the mind. The body remembers exactly what happened. The mind had to change its identity in order to survive. From these body memories, survivors can reconnect with the original pain, which in turn leads to the emotional truth of their experience.

Internalized Perpetrator/Persecutor

"Lies, lies. They're all lies. Look at you. You're disgusting. You're fat. No one will ever love you. You will never get out! It's too late. There is no hope. There is no way out."

As the pain increases, the voices of the perpetrators may be all the child can hear. The words become like knives tearing at his body. The more dizzy he becomes from the pain, the more the voices take on a hollow quality. The more dizzy he becomes, the more he forgets that the voices are coming from outside himself. Instead, he starts to hear them inside his head. He feels how the voices must be feeling. But he can't identify the voices. He feels all the bitter disgust and rage at himself that the voices are expressing. As the abuse continues, he finds himself being able to match the cruelty of the voices. Without thinking about it or knowing what it means, he winds up saying to himself all the same things the perpetrators say. It makes him feel strong and empowered to use such angry voices.

Even though he knows that the angry voices are against him in the moment, he doesn't exist as the child who is being hurt. Only the voices that make the child feel empowered and in control exist. He may find himself laughing with the perpetrators as he is being hurt. He is no longer the vulnerable child. He is powerful. He is one of them.

The personality that identifies with the abusers is called an *internalized perpetrator.* Hearing the hateful voices is almost like experiencing a hypnotic state for the child. If he agrees with the perpetrators, there is nothing to struggle against. This personality offers freedom from the pain during the trauma. It provides a numbing comfort that allows the child to stop feeling his own pain. Later, as this personality meets and speaks with other personalities, he realizes he was victimized and developed to empower the child. He chooses to direct his rage at those people who hurt him instead of at himself.

The Protectors

"I am going to kill them for this. Someday everyone
will pay for what they have done to me."

Protectors take care of the child at any cost. They will kill, maim, and torture, as long as the child can remain safe. They feel the rage and anger of the internalized perpetrators, but they know the cult is responsible for their pain. Protectors are the ultimate expression of self-love that is the guiding force behind the child's ability to survive. The protector provides the strength the child needs. When the child feels like caving in, the protector says, "He's an idiot. You are right. You are always right. Someday we will get him. You wait. In time." The protector takes care of the child. The protector matches the intense cruelty of the abusers to effectively ward off insults. This makes the child feel safe and strong. In adulthood, protectors are paramount to the survivor's ability to fight against both the abusers and a nonsupportive society.

As the personalities meet and talk with one another, they each realize more about the entire situation. The protector learns more information about what she can do to ensure the safety of the child. If the situation demands it, the protector learns there are ways out of the cult as an adult. The protector can decide that violence against others results in greater pain for the child in the long run; as a result, she will choose not to commit violent acts. Protectors are generally fair to those who are fair to them; but they will do what is best for the child without concern for anyone else. They are self-love usually guided by a sense of justice. They are the strength of the survivor.

Killers/Torturers

"Cut right there. Yes, one slice. Don't move. Again.
Aaah, the blood. Breathe. Taste it. This is the true
beauty of death."

The internalized perpetrators first learn to vent their rage and hostility onto the child. As time passes, the cult requires the child to vent the rage onto other innocent victims, but this task may be too difficult even for the internalized perpetrator. Originally, the child vents the rage on himself and doesn't have to deal with the guilt of hurting something or someone else. When the cult requires him to hurt others, the protector may step in to help the internalized perpetrator develop a new type of personality. This new personality embodies all the intense rage that results from the abuse and learns from the cult to direct this rage on other innocent victims. This personality is capable of killing, torturing, and maiming with no remorse. It is cold and calculating, and it may act on impulse and harm others for the mere pleasure of seeing someone suffer.

This personality is often a difficult one for both survivors and their support people to confront. It is easier to acknowledge self-hate than it is to accept that someone wants to brutalize an innocent victim. Furthermore, these killer personalities may borrow from the cult elaborate rationalizations to justify what they do. However, it is important to remember that the rationalizations are there to cover up the immeasurable pain the child originally experienced as he was forced to commit violent acts. The child stopped the pain by numbing out his feelings of compassion, guilt, or grief.

It is absolutely essential that the feelings and thoughts of these personalities are heard. The primary purpose of ritual abuse is mind control and indoctrination. The more people who are in the lie, the more the cults are able to justify what they do. Personalities who were "born" in the rituals are required to internalize the values and beliefs of the group. In order to do this, survivors often incorporate the cult teachings into their own innate beliefs and values. It is important not to discount any personality that expresses cultlike beliefs. The most powerful brainwashing techniques are designed to tap into the innate beliefs of survivors, making it very difficult to separate brainwashing from the victims' own personal truths. The group's values and beliefs are probably intertwined with the survivor's own belief system. In time, though, survivors are able to separate what they truly believe from what they were told as children about the world.

Acting on these violent impulses is not in the best interests of the system as a whole. These impulses are best curbed by protectors into words that can be heard by other personalities. This kind of communication protects these personalities by allowing them a safe, nonviolent way to express their anger. By finding words for their rage, these personalities are able to discover what circumstances in their lives are making them unhappy. When these personalities are completely ignored, the survivor cuts off her own inner radar that tells her when she feels violated by another human being. By listening to these personalities, the survivor allows herself to make changes to protect herself.

These personalities may believe that if they had been this strong when they were little, they never would have been hurt in the first place. They blame themselves for being too weak to protect themselves. They forget how small they were, and how much power adults have over children. No matter how hard and strong they learned to become inside, it doesn't change the fact that they were too little to escape and had to conform.

One of the most confusing aspects of the abuse for children is who to blame. If the children know that the adults who are abusing them are also being abused by others, they feel confused about who are the victims and who are the abusers. If they know that their parents were also ritually abused as children and have been trapped in the cult all their lives, then who is to blame for all this? Who is responsible? Children often end up blaming themselves because it stops the confusion. Even though there are a number of different types of adults in the cults—some who choose to be there and others who do not—the children are never responsible for what happened. Sometimes part of the grief is realizing just how helpless everyone has become.

Child Molester/Rapist

*"Come here, you little nasty. You have been a very
bad boy. I'm going to give you a little whipping now.
Pull down your pants."*

The association of violence and sex is a primary characteristic of ritual abuse. The cults persistently fondle the children's genitalia until the children's bodies physically react to the violating, abusive touch. Sometimes the sexual stimulation actually has a narcotic effect, reducing the physical and emotional pain.

Ritually abused children are surrounded by people who molest, torture, and rape people. They are continually taught rationalizations for why it is okay to hurt other people. The child may be told that the only way to be intimate with another creature is to be sexual with it. The child may grow up believing that the only way to be close to another human being is through sexual contact. As adults, these sexualized personalities may prefer sexual contact with children because they feel less vulnerable with children than with adults.

These personalities never learned that molestation and rape are wrong. They never learned that sexual abuse is one of the greatest betrayals of children's trust and adversely affects them for the rest of their lives. When they were molested, no one stopped what was happening. It wasn't "wrong" in the eyes of their abusers when it happened to them. These personalities grew up in an environment where all children are molested. These personalities may have no reference point other than the cult environment, and thus no other value system from which to operate. Just as personalities who live in the day-to-day world go for years without remembering the ritual abuse, the personalities who experience the abuse sometimes have no idea that they live another life outside of the cult. They may be amnesic of all the survivor's daily noncult experiences.

Other personalities within the system may feel deeply ashamed of the parts of themselves that enjoy hurting and molesting children. As the memories of these personalities surface, the survivors may feel so guilty for the feelings of these personalities that they become suicidal or homicidal. It is important to remember that the existence of these personalities was critical to the child's survival during the ritual abuse. These personalities had no choice but to be born. Only by listening to the truth of these personalities' experiences will survivors find relief. Talking about these personalities' feelings openly and honestly gives them a new ally other than the cult. If they are not listened to, these personalities will probably return to the only people who seem to accept them—the cult.

Intellectual

*"You were ritually abused. That is what it is called.
What you are feeling right now is pain from a
memory. They call it a body memory. Soon the pain
will stop."*

These personalities find words to stop the pain. They find labels and sort things into meaningful categories. These personalities are very intelligent. They figure out for the rest of the system the best action to take. They are the cool-headed personalities in the traumatic situation who can decide what to do next.

Children who are abused plan schemes in their minds for how they can get away. Their minds become wonderful playgrounds for tossing around ideas about their futures. This intellectual part exists only in the mind. It has no contact with the pain and rage of internalized perpetrators or protectors. Although it may be intellectually aware of what the abuse felt like, it feels no emotional connection to the original trauma. Hence, some of its decisions do not meet the needs of all personalities.

Guardian Angels, Helpers, Comforters, Nurturers

*"Breathe. Breathe. You will be safe. Hold on. It will
be over soon."*

Voices may also develop inside the child's mind to soothe the pain. As the abuse continues, the child is able to get free of the body and leave it behind. There is no pain from this place. The child floats above all that is happening below. A voice may say, "You are safe now. I won't hurt you. You can come with me and play if you like. There is a field over there where little children can play in the flowers and not be hurt."

All of this can take place right in the child's mind. The internal world is a protection from the brutality of the outer world. During the trauma, children reach out for a god or something greater than themselves that can stop the pain. They want something gentle and loving to comfort them. They don't want to be hurt. They want to be somewhere sweet where they don't have to hurt others.

These desires for goodness may be symbolized by "guardian angels"—voices that say, "I love you," when everyone around the child is being hurtful and mean. These voices may take on a magical, mystical element, which helps the child to feel more powerful than the cult. The idea of a pure good keeps many survivors from totally caving in and believing the lies of the cult. They remember what they really wanted out of life, and it is symbolized in these white-light personalities. Even though the protectors and internalized perpetrators may feel bitterly and horribly angry, these white-light personalities remind survivors that as children they only wanted to be loved.

These personalities are extremely contradictory to the violence of the cult. They take the child away from the cult to nice, safe places. These sweet, loving personalities found acceptance in the world, while the darker personalities were probably shamed and humiliated. The child probably learned that people liked her white-light personalities more than her angry ones. The child, wanting to be loved and understood by people, appreciated her white-light personalities more than the darker ones. Angry personalities who are not wanted or heard may bitterly resent these white-light personalities. At the same time, white-light personalities are often very invested in keeping the darker personalities a secret. They may allow the angry personalities to speak, but only if they learn the way of "goodness and righteousness."

Dangers arise from the dominance of white-light personalities. White-light personalities often have benevolent expectations of other personalities that they are unable to live up to. Also, the white-light personalities are not representative of the entire array of feelings experienced by a ritually abused child.

Ashamed of their own darker personalities, survivors may become judgmental and see "evil" in everyone else but themselves. Dominance of white-light personalities leaves survivors feeling hollow and empty. It also makes them vulnerable to people who act cruelly and maliciously. Survivors may at times live in a fantasy world, where they believe people don't hurt other people. Without protector-type personalities, survivors are vulnerable to people who are manipulative and untrustworthy. Without personalities who feel angry, they are unable to feel deeply empowered. In some cases, survivors alienate their darker personalities to such a degree that the personalities turn to the cult for comfort and understanding.

The Roles

Cults often assign specific roles to children. Some are temporary roles for a single ritual, but some survivors are groomed from childhood for specific adult roles. Some children, for example, are raised from infancy to be high priests or priestesses.

Taking on a specific role within the group may be similar to taking on a specific role in a play. Often the roles are designed to make survivors feel magical and powerful. These feelings may help survivors feel empowered in spite of the numerous attempts by the cult to disempower them. Identifying with their roles may be how survivors make spiritual connections to something higher than themselves. For this reason, some survivors may not want to give up their roles and leave the cult. Only when survivors have determined that the pleasure from the role is less than the pain caused by the cults will they find the courage to leave.

PERSONALITIES BORN OUTSIDE THE CULT

Some personalities develop outside the cult experience to help the ritually abused child function in the world. In spite of the child's deep suffering, these daily-life personalities learn never to feel the child's intense sorrow and anger. It was the sorrow and anger expressed outside of the cult that made the child seem different, and hence vulnerable to alienation from other children and adults. If the child felt her vulnerability, she risked ridicule from others. She had to smile with the other kids and laugh in spite of what was happening in secret. She learned never to think of the abuse. Soon this child had to give up the truth of her past. She had to forget. These daily-life personalities helped the child forget about the abuse. They learned to interact in a socially acceptable fashion with people outside of the cult experience. They internalized the norms and values of the noncult world in spite of the contradictory teachings they learned in the cult.

Ritually abused children want to keep the ritual abuse secret, while maintaining a sense of belonging with other children and adults. Children want to be liked, and the cult tells them no one will ever like them if they find out what they had to do in the cult. These personalities learn never to think about the abuse. By the time the children reach a certain age, these personalities are completely amnesic of the ritual abuse experience.

A strong amnesic split may also develop between personalities who deal with home, cult, and school. The child is able to juggle all these different ways of relating to the world by forgetting. While in the cult, he doesn't remember his life at school or with his family. While at school, he remembers nothing of the ritual abuse, and he remembers only the things about his home life that make him feel like the other children. He forgets about the physical and sexual attacks. As the child grows up, he may forget about all of the abuse in his childhood.

The nonremembering personalities outside of the trauma develop over time to meet the expectations and demands of the child's parents, teachers, and peers. These personalities are very distant from the feelings and memories of abuse. They can smile at Mommy and Daddy, even though they were molested the night before. They can even go to school after being ritually abused in the most humiliating manner possible. The more time that passes, the better these personalities become at forgetting and not feeling the emotions that result from the ritual abuse.

Most day-to-day personalities are invested in keeping the ritual abuse a secret. They no longer feel the pain of the abuse. They have survived. They may have learned to function in a world that values their "strength" and ability to endure pain. Conforming to our society took away their ability to freely express their pain about the ritual abuse. They don't want to acknowledge the weakness, rage, and hatred they may feel. If they were to acknowledge their hatred for the cults—and for the world that forced them to conform—they would have no place to belong. They would have no place that seemed safe and caring toward them.

These day-to-day personalities fear that if they ever felt the depths of their emotions, they would go crazy or disappear. In a way, they would disappear—another personality would emerge. Because remembering the ritual abuse often contradicts the memories and feelings of these day-to-day personalities, they might feel crazy as they remembered what happened.

The task of the personalities born after the initial trauma is to keep the child safe from pain or further victimization. Because the day-to-day personalities are usually unaware of the existence of other personalities, they feel overwhelming emotions that they can't account for in their present life. The seemingly unfounded emotions are other personalities starting to emerge. These personalities emerge in varying degrees. A personality may emerge merely as a thought, or it may completely take over the survivor's behavior. If the personality switch is abrupt, the survivor may lose time. Survivors often are able to prevent traumatized personalities from fully emerging and taking over their behavior by unconsciously calling on the personalities who have developed in the mind.

PERSONALITIES BORN IN THE MIND

Personalities who only exist in thoughts symbolize the survivors' chaotic and painful experiences, or the inexpressible pain of the ritual abuse. Survivors might refer to such personalities as the "devils" and "demons" that pursue them.

Other mental personalities symbolize the love survivors always needed from other people. The child may develop an elaborate fantasy world in her mind based on the dream of true love. Inside this fantasy world, she can symbolically confront her internal struggles and find the love she desperately needs. Survivors can control what happens in their fantasy worlds. In the real world—as children, and often as adults—they feel painfully helpless.

Some of the personalities who develop in the mind of the survivor never speak to "outside" people; they only speak to the survivor's other personalities. This is a powerful protection for mind-personalities: They can't be manipulated by anyone, since nobody knows they are there. They help the survivor cope with the pain and may explain to the survivor things other personalities cannot understand. They may provide each personality with needed information from other personalities about specific situations.

Some personalities act as go-betweens or messengers, making decisions about how much information can be shared between personalities. They keep cult memories separate from daily-life experiences. These personalities develop to meet two primary needs of the survivor: to survive and to belong. The survivor's first need is physical survival. The day-to-day personalities must be emotionally detached enough to function, to conform to society in a way that allows them to make enough money for food and shelter. Conforming requires these personalities to put the feelings and needs of traumatized personalities at bay. The personalities in the mind facilitate this process by making decisions about which personality is going to work.

Not surprisingly, when survivors remember the abuse and dissociation breaks down, they are unable to work. It is too difficult to have a memory of a brutal rape that includes all the emotions and physical sensations and then have to face coworkers with a smile. Unfortunately, most survivors are required to work while confronting memories. This makes it very difficult and painful for survivors to heal.

Second, the separation of cult memories from daily-life experiences fulfills the survivor's need to belong. The most painful feeling in the world is believing that no one is on your side. Survivors will do almost anything to keep from feeling so alone. For most ritual abuse survivors, being aware of the truth of their pasts also means realizing no one was on their side. Somewhere inside, they believe they will never be understood in a society that tends to minimize the problem of child abuse—and they know the cult won't stop hurting them—so they give up and ignore the reality of their predicament. They do what they have to do to make people like them. What they want or need as ritual abuse survivors becomes secondary to the needs of everyone else. In the worst case, the need to belong draws day-to-day personalities to situations reminiscent of the ritual abuse. They may join a cult that ritually abuses children, while remaining unaware of their own ritual abuse experience. When this happens, survivors have given up what they needed as children—love and protection—for this important sense of belonging with other people.

Personalities in the mind consistently try to help survivors meet these two basic needs. They try to weigh out the benefits and the costs. They choose what is best for the survivor in a given situation. Unfortunately, no matter what decision these personalities make, the needs of someone in the system will go unmet. Personalities who work to financially support the entire system must ignore the personalities who ache from head to toe with body memories from torture. Personalities who are angry at both the cult and society must be silenced if the survivor wants to belong. Personalities have to ignore one another, and even turn on each other if necessary, in order to meet these basic needs. This is a very painful reality for survivors of ritual abuse—a reality that can slowly be soothed, and possibly even changed, if the personalities learn to communicate.

COMMUNICATION AND COOPERATION

Communication exists between personalities even before survivors are aware that they are multiples. Personalities dream about one another. They talk to each other as the survivor falls asleep. Sometimes personalities talk to each other when the survivor is feeling emotionally overwhelmed. For example, a survivor driving down the street after an argument with her boss thinks to herself, "That little slimy scum. I am going to kill him. This is the last straw." The more she allows herself to think violent thoughts, the more she feels out of control. She feels if she continues allowing these thoughts, her mind will spin out of her head and she will disappear. She knows she will lose control of her behavior. Then a new voice emerges to stop these violent thoughts. "*You* need to be more understanding," the new voice says. "Just try to relax." While the first voice is raspy and angry, the second voice is soft and sweet. These two different thoughts emerge in the space of ten seconds.

The first indicator that these are personalities talking to one another is the use of the word "you" by one of the personalities. Multiples often talk to themselves by saying "you." They refer to the entire multiple system as "we." Usually, prior to the inner reflection that takes place during therapy, survivors are unaware of how they talk to themselves. Once they are aware of the other personalities, they are able to look back over their lives and see how they have often referred to themselves as "she," "he," "you," or "we."

As the personalities meet each other and speak with one another, they are able to more effectively meet the two primary needs of survival and belonging. Sometimes personalities will not have their needs met, but at least now they are allowed to speak. Their feelings and thoughts are heard even if survivors are unable to make changes to meet all their needs today. Survivors can do their best to see that the losing personality gets other important needs met. If all the personalities make a primary commitment to themselves, and not to pleasing others, no one has to be silenced any longer.

Once personalities are recognized and allowed to talk, they are no longer stuck in a time-warp, perceiving everything as reminiscent of the ritual abuse. Survivors see that their lives today are not half as brutal as they were as children. And if a survivor is still being brutalized today, the communication helps him realize there are ways to change the current situation. By waking up from the initial state of silence, the survivor is able to see that he does have choices today. He is able to choose who to have as friends. He is able to choose how he allows people to treat him. He can take every precaution to protect himself from further victimization.

One of the most painful aspects of ritual abuse is that survivors are forced to fragment their identities. Multiples are forced to be separate from themselves. They are lonely in the most devastating manner possible. They are lonely for themselves. During the healing process, survivors develop a way of treating themselves that they have yearned for their entire lives. They can find justice. They find unconditional love for their other personalities as they hear their own innocence and pain. They can be as codependent as they want to be with themselves. Some personalities can express their anger, and other personalities can listen to the pain. In time, the various personalities reach a point of deep, mutual respect.

All personalities want to be heard. They each hold a little piece of the survivor's personal truth. All the personalities together make up the survivor's reality. As the personalities listen to one another, they find common ground in their beliefs. Sometimes personalities express extremely contradictory thoughts and feelings, the result of having to meet the impossible demands of functioning in society while enduring such intense physical and emotional pain. Each personality is in place to help the system meet its basic needs; each deserves tremendous respect.

One personality never reveals the child's entire experience: Personalities born in the cult feel helpless and hopeless; comforter personalities do not feel the pain from their past. Communication allows each personality to see the system as a whole, to learn different perspectives. Communication makes the personalities feel more complete.

INTEGRATION

Integration allows survivors to effectively meet the needs of personalities. Instead of taking two hours to find out what the system as a whole needs in a given situation, integration allows survivors to know what all the personalities think, feel, and need without having to ask. Long-term, effective communication among personalities facilitates the process of integration. Personalities born in the day-to-day world integrate through the process of meeting and speaking with new personalities. They learn to respect each personality and the system as a whole. The personalities born in the trauma go back to their traumatic births to find what they lost inside of themselves at the moment they had to take on a new identity. Reliving the trauma in a safe, therapeutic process allows these personalities to feel whole again. The personalities born in the mind, no longer needing to keep everything separate, slowly integrate.

People who are deeply traumatized live in reaction to the trauma until they are able to heal. The process of healing is long and painful, especially in the case of ritual abuse. Finding someone who is able to hear the truth of the survivors' traumatic experiences is a difficult challenge. Survivors experience countless revictimizations until they find someone who is able to listen to what happened. Once they find someone, it takes years of support before the trauma stops affecting them on a daily basis.

Integration is not about getting rid of the sickness of multiple personality disorder. MPD is not what caused the pain. The pain is

about the trauma survivors experienced in the cult, and the alienation and abandonment they felt from a world that could not hear
their pain. Multiple personalities are what kept survivors from suicide or a mental hospital. The MPD helped the survivors meet the
demands of the world. It helped them protect themselves from further victimization. The personalities are not to blame for the pain
the survivors experience today. The cult that traumatized them and
the world that ignored and ridiculed them are the ones to blame.

Ritual abuse is an all-encompassing trauma. For many survivors, the abuse is as traumatic as for a child who sees his entire
family murdered in front of his eyes and yet people deny the murder happened. People never "just get over" extreme trauma. They
learn to live acknowledging their experiences. It may take years of
meeting and speaking with personalities before they integrate. Survivors may continue to find new voices within their minds for the
rest of their lives.

Survivors do have one clear choice: They can take back their
rights. They have the right to feel all the pain they experience inside.
They have the right never to want to speak to another human being
again. They have the right never to want to be a "good, productive
citizen" in a world where they were bitterly betrayed. They also have
the right and responsibility to respect the rights of others. In summary, they have the right to the feelings that resulted from the
abuse. They can rage and grieve about what happened. They can
take action to make their lives exactly how they want. They may
even choose to love and trust again. They can learn to trust the people who prove to be trustworthy. They won't own the shame of others. They take their own beliefs and opinions seriously. They
become their own best friends.

Chapter 3

Therapy for the Survivors

My first therapist taught me to play by the rules. He taught me what to say and what not to say. He helped me realize that I wasn't half as bad as people said I was. At the most hopeless point in my life, he was the person who kept me from killing myself.

My next therapist didn't know much about psychological theory. He operated from one assumption. He said I felt bad all the time because I couldn't control the people around me. In a way, he was right. I was miserable because I couldn't control other people. I couldn't make people stop being mean to me. I decided to give up on therapy.

When I decided it was time to confront my past, I went back into therapy hoping somebody had the answers that would soothe my pain. I didn't have any clear memories of the ritual abuse, but I had always known something really, really awful had happened to me in my childhood. In high school, I used to have flashbacks where I would feel overwhelmed with panic. I remember crying, "Oh, my God. Somebody get me out of here! Please, somebody help me! I'm going to die!" In junior high school, I used to wake up in the middle of the night literally paralyzed from fear. I never had an explanation for any of these things.

Also, I have been preoccupied with sex since I was five years old. I used to think I sexually acted out because I was dirty and messed up inside. That certainly was how I was treated by my parents and teachers when I sexually acted out. As an adult, I looked back on the sexual things I used to do as a small child and realized something. I knew more than any five-year-old should have ever known about sex. I knew about oral sex and intercourse. My vocabulary was filled with the most graphic terms for genitals and sexual acts. Where did

I learn these things? This realization started a whole new string of visits to therapists.

My next therapist wasn't interested in talking about my fears that I was sexually abused as a child. She told me I hated men. She even told me I liked to have sex because it made me feel like I had a penis. That was the last straw. I knew wanting a penis was not my problem. My problem was that I was miserable, and I wanted to know why.

Then I found a book, The Courage to Heal, a healing guide for sexual abuse survivors. Reading that book was like reading my life story. I never knew anyone else in the world felt as lonely and hurt as I felt. I realized I was not alone. Then the memories of the incest and ritual abuse surfaced. I started having flashbacks of abuse on a regular basis. My entire life fell apart. I couldn't keep the feelings down. My entire past was coming to a head.

My therapist at the time was well educated on the topic of sexual abuse. She was nice, and a great therapist for incest, but she couldn't handle the ritual abuse. She wasn't comfortable with the intensity of emotions, and she was unreliable. I would call her on Friday with an emergency, and wouldn't hear back from her until Monday. That was not acceptable for me during that critical time. I decided to move on.

Next I found a woman who knew a great deal about ritual abuse and multiple personalities. She seemed to be comfortable with all my feelings. She believed most of what I told her, but she couldn't believe certain things about my abuse that seemed to ruin her picture of the world. She identified me as the problem. I trusted her with so much of my past, and she stopped believing me when I needed her the most. I am sure she still believes I was just "fantasizing" certain details of the abuse. I terminated the therapy.

Finally, I started to see the woman I am with today. When I first met her, I felt threatened. She was excessively nice—too nice, in my book. She had a soft, sweet voice. I figured there was something wrong with her. I thought she was denying her own rage.

I took it slowly with her, waiting for her to say something abusive. I waited for her to make a little cutting comment when I felt vulnerable. Nearly all the therapists I had seen before would make such comments. I thought all people felt a need to hurt people who were vulnerable. That is practically all I have seen, both in the cult and in the world. But this woman was to change my view.

Even when she feels angry, she carefully chooses her words to make sure that she doesn't hurt me. She consistently tells me that her commitment to me in therapy is to hear my feelings. If she has feelings that come up while we are together, she says it is her responsibility to find out where the feelings are coming from inside of her. She doesn't blame me for her feelings of discomfort. She doesn't think I am shameful. I think even if she did think something mean, she would deal with it without trying to hurt me. This is how she lives her life. She is a genuinely caring person who truly believes in the child inside of everyone, the child who wants love.

I have seen God knows how many therapists. I have put up with a lot of bullshit. Almost everyone I met in my life felt a need to control me. But this woman just lets me be. I spend our therapy sessions telling her exactly what I need to say. She doesn't have an agenda. My personalities come up when they want to say something, and she doesn't label anything. I talk, and she listens and lets me know that she understands. And when she doesn't understand, she usually asks me to elaborate. Most of all, she is honest.

I think she really cares about me. Not because I pay her money, but because the way that she gives has made me be the best person I can possibly be when I am with her. This doesn't mean I say nice things. In fact, I tell her all the mean things I think and do, and she hears the feelings behind the actions and acknowledges them and supports me. She always makes me feel heard.

Looking for a good therapist is like looking for a best friend. Don't settle for a therapist just because he or she claims to be an expert. Don't settle for a therapist just because he or she says you need to learn how to trust people. If a therapist is making you feel uncomfortable you might want to switch therapists. Don't let someone tell you it is "your process issues" that are making you feel bad about the therapy and that you need to stay until you see things from his or her perspective. Don't let a therapist tell you that your discomfort is not justified. Trust your feelings. If you don't trust your feelings, how will your feelings ever be heard? And if they are never heard, how will you ever find happiness?

Many people search for that special person who will listen to all their secrets without judging them. Often we are unable to share all of our thoughts and feelings with our friends or lovers. Everyone is influenced by societal expectations to deny certain types of feelings; and often our most vulnerable feelings are not listened to or judged. In therapy many people find the needed safety that allows them to share the hidden thoughts they share with no one else.

Effective therapy for ritual abuse survivors allows them the chance to finally be heard. It offers survivors a chance to focus on their needs and wants without having to worry about the reactions of other people. Therapy is a unique relationship because clients don't have to spend half the session talking about their therapists' problems at home. The focus is solely on the feelings and thoughts of the clients.

THERAPEUTIC STAGES

Therapy is a relationship survivors must enter into with caution. For survivors of ritual abuse, therapy is almost always the first time another human being has made a commitment to listen to the details of the ritual abuse. Sometimes survivors tell the truth of their experience only to be judged or not believed. Sadly, survivors are frequently revictimized by therapists and other professionals. This makes it very difficult for them to seek help in the future. However, if survivors are persistent, often they are able to find therapists who are knowledgeable about ritual abuse. Some survivors even find therapists who are willing to listen and believe the entire truth of their ritual abuse experiences.

Most ritual abuse survivors develop MPD as a result of the trauma. The therapy process described outlines the standard framework for therapy for ritual abuse survivors with multiple personalities.

Establishing Trust

During the first stage of therapy, therapist and client establish a bond of trust. If the client is not aware of the multiplicity, the therapist tells the client of the probability of multiple personalities and allows the client time to process this new information.

Colin Ross, a well-known authority on MPD, speaks of the importance of developing trust with the MPD client:

> The therapist develops trust by being trustworthy....
> It is important to remember that the MPD patient has had
> her trust in loved ones violently broken countless times.
> She has developed a complicated system of protectors,
> persecutors, and other personalities to deal with problems of
> trust and safety: The total personality system simply won't
> accept "caring" statements about how much the therapist
> can be trusted.

Ross notes the importance of validating the personalities who do not trust. He agrees with these personalities that it is smart not to trust all people, but he also reminds the client that some people can be trusted.[1]

The issues surrounding ritual abuse are complex, and it is important for the therapist to allow the survivor to decide just who can be trusted. It is not useful for therapists to suggest that their clients blindly trust them. As in all relationships, the survivor needs a great deal of time to evaluate and determine whether the therapist is trustworthy. Survivors of ritual abuse learned at a very young age not to trust a person just because he or she is in a position of authority or in a "helping" profession. Many survivors report having been abused by such individuals.

Developing Communication and Cooperation

During the next stage of therapy, therapists attempt to speak with alter personalities. They help survivors develop tools to aid in the process of personality communication and cooperation. Therapists generally attempt to establish verbal or written commitments with self-destructive, suicidal, or homicidal personalities before beginning the process of uncovering memories of abuse. It is essential that therapists learn to communicate effectively with their MPD clients.

Communication between therapists and MPD clients can be complicated by a number of factors. First, therapists must remember that clients with MPD do not always know what their other personalities think or feel. Multiples often contradict themselves inadvertently, confusing their therapists. Nevertheless, the therapist can address the entire personality system if important information needs to be communicated to everyone. Second, it is important to remember that all personalities can hear what the therapist is saying. Therefore, to slander one personality in the presence of another would create conflict and pain in the multiple. All personalities developed for survival purposes, and each still serves a purpose today. The personalities are an elaborate system that helped survivors live through extremely painful and traumatic experiences. Therapists need to treat clients with respect.

Frank Putnam, author of *Diagnosis and Treatment of Multiple Personality Disorder,* notes a specific type of personality found in most multiple systems who is capable of facilitating the process of communication between therapist and client. This personality, often referred to by therapists as an Internal Self Helper (ISH), is able to communicate the needs, desires, and wishes of the system as a whole. Therapists have found that establishing trust with this personality early in therapy aids the process of healing. The ISH is often very protective of other personalities; it can serve as an extraordinary helper, assuring that all personalities are heard and that all needs are met throughout the process of therapy.[2] Empowering and validating the reality of all the personalities is also essential throughout the process of therapy.

Developing communication and cooperation among all personalities is a vital step in the healing process. The therapist can aid in this process by pointing out common ground among personalities. When the barriers among the personalities are softened, they are able to feel closer together. Communication and cooperation aid in the development of a new understanding, which results in a greater sense of relief for the survivor. When each personality is able to have his or her needs met, this ends the battle among personalities for control of the survivor's behavior.

Once the personalities begin to communicate and cooperate, boundaries among personalities begin to dissipate. The separate reality of each personality leaks into the reality of the others. As this happens, survivors become plagued with memories of abuse and often experience overwhelming suicidal or homicidal impulses. It is essential to develop both internal and external safety for ritual abuse clients as they remember the abuse. Most therapists and clients achieve this through the use of commitments that assure survivors will not hurt themselves or someone else as the memories surface. Commitments can be made either among the personalities themselves, or among the personalities and the therapist. Each survivor is able to decide which type of commitment is the most useful in his or her individual situation.

Therapy for ritual abuse survivors is often a long and painful process that involves uncovering horribly traumatic memories. Most survivors experience these memories during what is referred to in psychological terms as an *abreaction*. During an abreaction, survivors feel all the physical sensations and emotions they had at the time of the abuse. Survivors of ritual abuse report the same process of abreaction as described with regard to sexual abuse by Ross:

> During an abreaction the child alter may beg the parent to stop, scream, cry, express intense sadness, or clutch her lower abdomen. There may be hand movements to push the father out of her vagina or motor movements accompanying the abreaction of an oral rape. The genuineness and the intensity of the abreaction is one of the most convincing features of MPD. For the therapist it is almost like having to watch a real rape, and then talk with the victim afterwards.[3]

THE MEMORY PROCESS

The memory process described by ritual abuse survivors is remarkably similar to the memory process described by war veterans and incest survivors. As people are severely traumatized, the violent memories become frozen in time. Later, after the danger has ceased, the victims recall the trauma in their bodies through unidentifiable physical sensations. They may have recurrent aches in their arms and legs. In the case of sexual abuse, they feel sharp pains in their vagina or rectum. They may be plagued with visual flashes of the violence. Most victims experience flashbacks in which their entire bodies and minds actually react as if they were back in the traumatic moment. The victims feel all the physical sensations and emotions they felt when the trauma occurred. The violence and pain seem to be happening all over again.

According to the men and women who volunteered for the research project on which this book is based, the memory process is extremely painful, both emotionally and physically. Most survivors said the memories surfaced in fragments. Initially, for example, survivors often experience body memories—physical sensations in their bodies with no current cause. The sensations experienced during the body memories are literally the body reliving the pain it felt during the trauma. During or after the body memories, the emotions emerge that they felt during the attack. Survivors often see flashes in their minds of abusive episodes that seem related to the feelings and body memories they are experiencing. As these memory fragments fall into place, the entire abusive event is then recalled as if the event was happening at that very moment.

Some survivors report that their alter personalities tell them the memories of abuse. Sometimes survivors experience feelings related to the abuse, which they are unable to account for in their daily lives. One ritual abuse survivor reported having intense sexual feelings associated with violence, and later feeling baffled that she would ever think such things. This is a somewhat common experience for ritual abuse survivors: The personality who felt sexually stimulated learned the association of sex and violence during the ritual abuse. The other personality was baffled because such feelings are unacceptable to her and don't feel like her own.

One survivor related that she could stop the physical and emotional pain experienced during the memory process by letting another personality who feels no pain take over. Survivors may use this dissociative technique to help ease the pain when a memory is surfacing in an unsafe environment.

Most survivors say there is an initial object, situation, or sensation—often referred to by survivors as a *trigger*—that begins the process of the memory. According to survivors, if they can identify the trigger, the memory process is shorter in duration and less painful. One survivor illustrates her process of memory recovery in great detail:

Getting a memory is not always an unbroken journey from point A to point B, but the process has taken on a consistency and familiarity that now helps me (and my support providers) jump in and manage the emergence of information. I think the process I endure is complicated by several factors: (1) whether or not I've been exposed to a specific trigger or cue, either deliberately (communication from a family member) or incidentally; (2) if I am vulnerable to being overwhelmed by repressed memories because of the time of year or a full moon; (3) if outside, normal life events are causing me to experience feelings that are connected to memories of the abuse; or (4) if there has been specific programming put into me in childhood that is causing me to react to a life event such as a specific birthday or holiday.

If I've been exposed to a specific trigger, the process feels a little simpler to me, especially if it has been an incidental trigger and not a deliberately placed one. Example: I saw a pair of earrings on a woman at a party; I didn't connect it at the time, but I later realized it was the exact moment I started feeling "concussed," as if I'd suffered a dizzying blow to the head. I left the party and went home feeling "fogged out," unconnected, unreal, distant, forgetful, "crowded," overwhelmed. (Sometimes I hear from "inside people" at this time, kids usually, who know something about the event I am fighting to keep from consciousness.) I then started to feel complete despair, hopelessness, and futility. I wanted to die. I didn't want to live. I couldn't live. I thought of my blood running out onto the floor. I felt anguish, terror, a feeling of unavoidable impending punishment and doom. I tried to manage the feelings while also attempting to trace back to the original trigger, and got support from my husband. I finally got the memory, hours after the party. I held onto my husband and got flooded with feelings of terror, horror, nausea, and grief. The earrings were tiny ceramic deer heads (something I had not remembered until then). The memory was about having to help my father disembowel and dismember a deer in a public restroom at a national park, and having

to make satanic symbols in blood on the walls, floor and
ceiling. I cried and shook and held on, swore I didn't believe
any of it, swore I was "crazy and manipulative," and cried
some more. My husband kept reassuring me, telling me he
believed me, reminding me that I was experiencing intense,
uncontrollable emotion, feelings he knew I could not and
would not fake. Once it passed, I felt enormous relief. I felt
clearheaded again, and I no longer wanted to die or harm the
body. But I did feel a lot of grief and sadness and anger at
being used, which required several more days to work
through, and a whole lot more tears.

If the trigger has been deliberately delivered to me (a
birthday card from my father, for example); or if it's a satanic
holiday or a full moon; or if I'm experiencing a lack of
confidence or support; if I'm experiencing stress at work
or in my relationship; or if I'm reacting to previously
programmed information, recovering a memory gets a little
more complicated. I have a much harder time "catching the
association," and a much more difficult time believing I am
a ritual abuse survivor in the first place. The denial is
excruciating. But there generally is always a transition from
being concussed, and feeling dead or nonexistent, to being
flooded with intense feelings of terror, dread, unbearable
shame, self-contempt, anger, and confusion (all in no
particular order). I no longer act out as frequently as I used
to, but the incredible urge to self-mutilate is frequently still
there. I frequently have to struggle with intense suicidal
feelings, and long, horrible bouts of panic. I've learned,
though, that all this hoopla, the suicidal feelings, the panic,
the intense self-hatred, the scathing hostility that too many
good and safe people get barraged with, the confusion and
hopelessness and despair, are usually just a complicated
"cover-up" for the emerging memory. Once I can get
somewhere safe, and experience the terror as fully as I can
stand it (this frequently entails having to "let go of the body"
and "accept the memory from whomever is holding it"), and
get as many details as I can about what actually happened,
and then get supported and comforted and reassured (as well

as gently corrected, if I'm steadfastly insisting that "I deserve to die" or "It was all my fault"), I typically experience immediate and profound relief. My "post memory" state can include anything from an incredible feeling of lightness and relief, to a mind-numbing heavy grief, to a blinding rage at my perpetrators, but I always feel better—less controlled by outside forces, less pursued, less off-balance and confused, less crazy.

I should also mention that at varying stages of this process before, during, and after a memory, I frequently experience intense physical pain: the sensation of a thin metal wire being inserted into my urethra; the sensation of pins being pushed in my nipples, the maddening sensation that my ankles or wrists are tightly bound (Until I figured that one out, I kept insisting, "It feels like my feet are being cut off." My feet obviously were never cut off, but if the circulation is impaired, that is in fact the physical sensation); the feeling of being "torn apart" by a rape, or "being ripped in two" (feeling a bodily sense of physically being very small); the feeling of being crushed or confined in a very small cage, or buried (including, on one occasion, the sensation that my fingernails were torn and bloodied from scratching uncontrollably on the lid of the coffin); or the sensation that the tips of my fingers are cut, burned, or crushed. But again, once the memory becomes more conscious, I always feel some relief, even if it takes a while to manifest. The ankle memory in particular just about drove me nuts: night after night after night, I couldn't sleep without tying socks around my ankles because the sensation of them being cut off was so strong. That one still comes and goes, but at least I have a context for it now. It is far worse to be suffering and have no way to process it, no way to explain it or endure it.

THE FOUR PHASES OF MEMORY RECOVERY

The process of recovering a memory generally goes through four phases. In phase one, the survivor feels anxious, nauseated, and panicky; in phase two, fragments of memory return; phase three is abreaction; and phase four is relief.

Phase One: Anxiety, Nausea, Panic

Many survivors are able to identify certain feelings that let them know a memory is surfacing. One survivor described this initial sensation "as a black presence coming over me." Other survivors reported mounting anxiety and feelings of nausea or fatigue. Some survivors said they felt a strong desire to revert to addictive behaviors. They wanted to start smoking again or out-of-control eating. Some individuals started to feel foggy or experienced irritating headaches. They felt they couldn't think. These feelings are a glimpse of how survivors felt during the original trauma.

Most of the feelings experienced by survivors as the memory surfaces are body memories. The body is experiencing what it felt during the abuse, but the mind is unable to identify why the body is feeling the pain. It is not uncommon for survivors to experience suicidal feelings or desires to self-mutilate as the memory surfaces. The pain and anxiety survivors experience as memories emerge is often so great that suicide seems like the least painful solution. The suicidal feelings may also be body memories of how they felt when the abuse was happening. Death might have seemed comforting to a child being tortured.

A numb, dead feeling may also accompany the suicidal impulses. For example, a survivor goes into shock during physical trauma, which causes a numb sensation throughout the body. When the memories return, the survivor experiences a heavy, numb sensation that creates great discomfort. Inflicting cuts on his own body may cause enough pain to seem to stop the numb feeling. However, the numb feeling is a body memory that will reemerge unless the survivor looks at the source of his feelings. If he can ride the numb feeling out without cutting his wrists, the entire memory may surface, which results in freedom from the pain. If he doesn't ride it out, and instead acts on his urges to self-mutilate, he continues the cycle of pain his abusers caused.

It is extremely important for a ritual abuse survivor to be in a safe environment as the memories surface. This might be extremely difficult if the survivor is in an unsupportive relationship or work environment. One of the most important aspects of healing from such extreme trauma is finding a safe place. The survivor needs to confront memories in order to recognize and grieve about losses, and for the past to no longer control the present. Finding a safe place may be a challenging task. No place feels safe to a survivor of ritual abuse. That in and of itself is part of the memory. No place was safe as the abuse was happening. Survivors can call on nontraumatized personalities (the ones who do not remember the pain and fear), and personalities who are aware of how the cults work, to help determine when and where it is safe for memories to emerge.

Because the pain is so intense as the memories surface, survivors must take certain precautions. If the memory starts to surface while the survivor is not in a safe place, they might comfort the pain by expressing feelings through writing or artwork. Sometimes talking about the surfacing feelings will ease the discomfort. Some survivors use peaceful imagery or desensitization techniques to distance themselves from the overwhelming material. Later, when they are in their safe place, they are able to remember the abuse, with all the feelings it entails.

Having to repress memories as they emerge in unsafe environments is one of the most difficult aspects of remembering the abuse. In time, however, survivors find safe places where their feelings are heard. They learn how to ride out the feelings without taking the pain out on their own bodies.

Phase Two: Uncovering Pieces of the Memory

After survivors are able to get through the initial feelings of anxiety, panic, and dread, they enter into stage two of the memory process. At this point, survivors get information or pieces of the memory without fully reliving the abusive experience. Some survivors see in their minds scenes of abuse as they encounter the initial trigger emotions. Often they have nightmares or flashes of abuse in dreams. At this stage in the memory process, survivors describe different layers of feelings, emotions, visualizations, and other details about the memory that must be integrated in order to relive the memory in its entirety. In therapy, survivors attempt to contact the inner personalities who have more information about the surfacing memory. Some survivors work with their therapists, going over and over a specific memory until all emotions, body memories, and visualizations combine to create a complete memory of an abuse episode.

Most survivors said therapy was their safe place. Therapists generally teach survivors relaxation exercises to ease the survivors' minds. This allows personalities who are not usually allowed to speak the opportunity to emerge. Some therapists use formal hypnosis, although this may not be necessary because many individuals with MPD are able to self-induce hypnosis. Hypnosis allows people to enter an altered state. Multiples often are able to move in and out of altered states with great ease.

Once the client is in a relaxed state, the therapist usually asks questions about the mental images the client is seeing, or feelings the client might be experiencing. Often survivors see old abuse scenes or remember the details surrounding an abuse episode. The therapist then asks such questions as, "How did you get here? Do you hear any sounds? Who is around you? What are you feeling?" Often these questions prompt more images, which later result in a memory of an abuse scene that includes all the feelings and sensations that accompanied the original incidence of trauma.

During this information-gathering stage of the memory process, it is not unusual for survivors to struggle with the images and feelings associated with a variety of abuse memories that share a particular theme. For example, the theme might be, "Don't tell about the abuse," and the survivor sees images of herself being tortured as a child. She may also have feelings associated with a memory as a teenager, when she told a friend at school her father had molested her and she was ostracized by her peers. Sometimes, if the common theme of the emerging memories can be identified, it is easier to process and express the emotions.

As the memory process continues, the images become more solidified and they combine with emotions and other details of the abuse to create a complete memory that includes all the feelings and sensations the survivor experienced at the time of attack. The original images often are the framework for an entire memory that is remembered, in the same way war veterans remember trauma on the battlefield. At the final stage of the memory process, survivors know their memories are true as clearly as they know their own name. They feel it in every cell of their bodies because they are literally reliving the experience.

It is important that survivors feel safe as pieces of memories surface. This is difficult because, as the memory is uncovered, survivors often lose conscious awareness of their behavior for short periods of time. In order to assure that all personalities feel safe, therapists and clients often establish commitments with personalities who may either hurt their own bodies or their therapists. These violent personalities hold all the suffering and rage of the client and endure the excruciating pain that has never been expressed. They need to be treated with respect. This means the violent personalities need to be allowed the safety of not acting on their feelings, because doing so could result in further traumatization of the system as a whole.

Each time a survivor attempts to remember the details of an abuse memory, it is useful for the therapist or survivor to read a commitment designed to protect the survivor from hurting herself or others. The following is an example of a commitment between personalities:

> We are going to a very important place now, where you are going to find parts of yourself you may have thought were no longer with you. In order for this to happen, your other personalities need to know that all of you can keep yourselves safe. They need to know that you won't hurt me or yourself. You have this object [perhaps a stuffed animal] that you can pretend to hurt, but it is not safe to hurt real people. If you can all agree with this, let's go further. Is this okay with you?

If the personalities agree with this, the therapist may want to add that an adult personality will need to come back into the body at a later point in the therapy session in order for the survivor to get home safely. For example, after the client agrees to the above commitment, the therapist may say,

> Okay. We have X amount of time to find these personalities and talk with them. After this time is up, an adult personality

needs to know that she or he will be able to come back into the body to get all of you home safely. If you all can agree with this, let's go further. Is that okay with you?

This statement is necessary to assure that personalities will be able to function as they leave the office and not feel overwhelmed. If the personalities do not agree with these commitments, then therapist and client may want to discuss why. Hopefully, they can arrive at compromises that allow all personalities to have their needs met.

For example, a personality may not agree to these commitments because she is afraid the therapist will attack her if she lets another personality surface. This personality is probably a child who was attacked countless times and needs to be assured that the therapist is safe and nonviolent. In the cult, survivors were often tortured for remembering and telling. A great deal of time may pass before all personalities feel safe enough to remember details of the abuse.

Phase Three: Abreaction

As therapists and survivors continue to explore pieces of the memory—and as survivors more clearly recall the details of the abuse—survivors enter stage three of the memory process. In this stage, survivors recall the abuse as if it was happening right in that moment. As they feel all the emotions and see the images of abuse, they recognize that this is not the first time they have experienced these feelings and physical sensations. They know they are remembering events that actually occurred years ago. Finding out the truth of their past is the answer to all the unidentifiable pain they have experienced their entire lives.

Therapists call this third stage of the process an abreaction. Survivors who experience abreactions feel as if they are right there, and the abuse is happening all over again. Here's how one survivor describes the process:

> When an alter has a memory, it is in flashbacks. We are back at that moment in time. We can see the people involved clearly; we can feel them, smell them, taste them, and hear them. We were able to stop our feelings from showing by locking the pain inside. Our body moves as though someone

is hurting it. If we are involved in a rape, the body is pushed as though someone is on top of us having intercourse. The breath is knocked out of us. The whole body stiffens in defense. Sometimes there is spontaneous bleeding. There is intense fear. Now that the child alters trust the therapists, they can tell them what's happening and cry and ask for help, something they never did when it really happened.

Nearly all the survivors in this study report a similar memory process. Often survivors find validation for the images they see during the memory of abuse. One survivor in this study said that after an abreaction, she found a scar she had never noticed before in the same place from which the pain was coming during the abreaction. Another survivor said she started to hemorrhage in the middle of the memory. The memories of some survivors are verified by other people who were abused at the same place and time. Some survivors visit the location of the abuse scene they saw in their memory and find it to be identical to the image they saw in their memory.

Phase Four: Relief

After an abreaction, survivors report feelings of relief. The struggle to stop the pain is diminished. They confronted the pain, and it passed. Survivors said they felt tremendous relief as they "let go of control of their bodies" and allowed the personalities that held the memories to emerge. Memories become easier to process as survivors are able to make the association between the trigger, the overwhelming feelings, and the surfacing of a ritual abuse memory. When they do not realize a memory is surfacing, they are unable to identify why they are feeling such powerful emotions. Their emotions feel out of their control.

Throughout the healing process, it is essential for survivors to be aware of their child personalities who are suffering and need to be heard. Nurturing these children is an important part of the healing process. Letting these little children play or do something they deem enjoyable helps to remind survivors that there is more than just the pain of the memories. If survivors do not know what the child personalities want, it is useful to ask. If there is no answer the first time, just keep trying. It may take a while to find the personalities who feel safe enough to search for fun.

Reparenting the inner children allows survivors the opportunity to take control of their lives. Since most multiples were abused by their parents, child personalities only know about unfair and cruel parents. These child personalities now have a chance to be reparented by the most kind and fair personalities in the multiple system. These children are able to have their needs heard. They are respected. These inner children give survivors the lives rooted in their hearts that they thought were lost forever. Reparenting the inner children is about being the best parent you can possibly be to yourself.

For survivors, the most rewarding part of healing is developing a relationship with themselves. They learn to understand the feelings and behavior of alter personalities. Supporting these alter personalities may be difficult at times, but eventually all personalities are able to have a voice. They are finally heard. Allowing certain personalities to speak may cause a great deal of anxiety in survivors, as they hear the contradictions in their thoughts and behavior. Core beliefs of certain personalities are questioned by other personalities. In time, however, survivors develop compassion for each personality. Personalities are respected. They are allowed to change their minds and make mistakes. In the end, everyone is recognized and heard.

USING MULTIPLE PERSONALITIES TO HEAL FROM RITUAL ABUSE

> Multiple personalities is not only a creative way to survive a childhood which was awful, but it's also a very creative way to heal. And I think if you use multiplicity as part of your healing process and work with it rather than against it, then you can actually experience multiplicity as a healing thing.
>
> M. M., *Healing Hearts*[4]

Multiplicity originally enabled survivors of ritual abuse to live through highly traumatic situations. Multiplicity also offers gifts for survivors as they heal from the abuse. Survivors remember many memories of severe trauma with the same intensity of feeling they experienced at the time of the abuse. By working with the multiplicity, adult survivors recover these memories at a pace that doesn't overwhelm them. Multiples can also learn to develop internal support that helps them survive this painful process.

A Word to the Survivor: Multiple to Multiple

A wonderful thing happens as you take the time and energy to meet and speak with inner personalities. You start to see your own innocence and feel the feelings you were never allowed to express. You find the parts of yourself that are sweet and the parts that are powerful. All of your parts make up an incredibly unique, creative individual who did everything in her or his power to survive. You start to see your own uniqueness and feel warmth and compassion toward yourself. You may even fall in love with yourself, which is a remarkable experience when you realize that all these cute, lovable, powerful things inside of you are really you.

As you discover alter personalities, it may prove useful to keep some sort of a map that outlines relationships between personalities and the characteristics of each that you believe are important. Be creative. It is your system, and you know best how to express what needs to be said. Allow the personalities to speak, and feel them. Let them communicate with you.

Communication allows personalities to talk to each other about what they think, believe, and feel. Some techniques you can use to communicate with personalities include journaling and allowing parts to write back and forth; coloring or drawing the memories or images personalities want to share; or actual communication within the mind that allows parts to engage in discussions. There are many ways to communicate with alter personalities. You may find that communication already exists between personalities, but you were not consciously aware of it. It is essential to find the most comfortable form of communication for each personality. Systems can be very intricate and specialized. Some say that there are as many different multiple systems as there are multiples. Trust what feels right to you.

Here are some questions that may prove useful as you meet each alter personality:

- What is your name? (not all personalities will have names)
- How old are you?
- When were you born?
- Why were you born?
- What needs of the overall system did you meet at the time you were born?
- What needs do you meet now?
- What happened before and after your birth?
- How do you feel about yourself? About other parts in the system?
- What do you know about our life and what happened to us?
- Who else do you know or talk to in the system?
- What do you need from the rest of the system?
- How do you feel about the outside world?
- What can we do to help you? to make you feel safe?
- Do you perceive yourself as related to any other personalities?
- What do you look like?
- What do you hate?
- What do you love?
- Is there anything important that you need to tell me?

It may be particularly frightening to begin communication with certain personalities, if you know that what they will share may hurt you. These personalities may hold painful memories. They may resent you or may be angry at you. They may want to hurt someone you love. Nevertheless, these personalities are altered states of yourself that have been extremely abused and need the support, love, and understanding you never received. Take it slowly, and do the best you can. You may be able to make deals with them. If you can't communicate with a personality because you need to do something else at that time, try to explain why the job that needs to be done is important. You may even realize that what you thought was important can wait, and you can now take a little time out and listen to what is going on inside. Generally, if you treat personalities with respect, they will be respectful in return.

The group as a whole may want to design guidelines that enable each other to be heard. You can have family meetings each night to discuss the hardships of the day or to decide what you need to do tomorrow and who is going to do it. This may feel uncomfortable initially, but it is remarkable how much anxiety is released once you acknowledge alter personalities. This makes sense once you consider that these personalities are altered states of yourself; they influence you and they are with you at every moment.

The system can assign different personalities to different jobs to make each day run more smoothly. Find out what each personality likes to do. You can view the system as a large family or commune—helper personalities meet responsibilities and get work done, nurturer personalities hold babies who are crying and in severe pain. Babies may also like to be with protector personalities, who can hold their hands or give them tough-guy lessons. It is important to remember that each personality has something to offer another personality and the system as a whole. The trick is to find out what that is, and to make up for lost time. The process is unique to each multiple system, and I encourage survivors to use the cooperation tactics that work best for them.

Personalities may be hostile and angry if they have been ignored for most of your life. If other parts hated them or were ashamed of them, they may feel resentful and not want to take part in any process that may help all of you. At such times, it is important to remember the enormity and the injustice of your ritual abuse experience. Many, many times, these personalities are right. You are right. Give the personalities all the things that were never given to you. They were violently violated, and they need someone—they need *you*—to understand. In time, you will feel closer to your personalities. As you start using tools to develop cooperation within the system, you will feel better each day. You may even stop perceiving differences between them and you. Your beliefs and their beliefs are the same. You feel what they feel. The congruency in thought and emotion is miraculous.

Meeting personalities and uncovering memories requires an intense commitment to listening and understanding *all* parts in the multiple system. Personalities often hold all the horrible, awful feelings you were never allowed to feel as a child, and they burn with pain as a result of it. For this reason, as the memories and feelings surface, it is ideal to have supportive individuals around you to help you reach into the depths of your pain; outside people who are able to listen to what your parts need to say and are not afraid of them or their experiences. This may be the most difficult part of recovery—finding people with whom your personalities feel safe; people who will listen to all of your experiences without attempting to discount or minimize your feelings. This frustration and lack of support may justifiably cause you to be sensitive to other people's controlling behaviors to minimize your pain and experience. You may also become furious at society for its mistreatment of victims. You may feel isolated in your suffering. But you are not alone. Remember, other survivors are out here right now, going through the same process. Keep looking until you find someone outside of yourself who can hear the truth and be there for you.

Overcoming Self-Destructive Impulses

It is not uncommon for survivors to experience extreme self-destructive and homicidal impulses as memories surface. At this time, it is important to remember that you are not to blame for what happened, and you deserve to remember and recover your own life. You are experiencing normal reactions to a very abnormal, abusive experience. Being reminded of your own worth may help lessen the drive to act on these self-destructive feelings. Sometimes it is because of a surfacing memory that you are experiencing such moments of depression and self-destruction. Ride the feelings out. Don't give in and hurt your own body. You've already come this far. Things are going to change. Remember, you are not to blame for what happened to you, and you deserve to remember the abuse and heal.

The Rewards of Healing

Healing from ritual abuse is about learning to live with what happened to you. It requires you to feel the feelings people never allowed you to express. In order for you to find out your true feelings, you must listen to your alter personalities. As you communicate and cooperate with your personalities, their distinctiveness will become less apparent. In time, personalities may no longer be separate from the person you are in your daily life, a process called *integration*. When you integrate, you know what your personalities think and feel without having to ask.

It is my opinion that integration is not a goal of healing, but rather the result of it. In fact, maintaining integration as a goal may actually hinder healing if it encourages certain personalities to remain silent in order to please other personalities or their therapist.

The healing process is not as simple as regurgitating memories over a finite number of years. What you have now is the chance to learn more about yourself and to reach inside and find a rich, whole world that can give you back your life. Memories are only part of the process. Discovering what is really important to you, and finding your strengths and your own place in this world, are only some of the rewards you receive for undertaking the long and hard process of healing. Even though the new communication between alters is usually accompanied by horrible childhood abuse memories, multiples have a unique opportunity to act as a support system and nurturer for themselves. Personalities can help one another, hold one another, and work in their internal environment to create a world inside that feels comfortable and supportive to everyone. The process may appear long and tedious, but the rewards are well worth it.

NOTES

1. Colin Ross, *Multiple Personality Disorder: Diagnosis, Clinical Features, and Treatment* (New York: John Wiley & Sons, 1989), 220.

2. Frank Putnam, *Diagnosis and Treatment of Multiple Personality Disorder* (New York: The Guilford Press, 1989), 203.

3. Ross, *Multiple Personality Disorder,* 113.

4. *Cooperation Versus Integration* (1989) and *Maintaining Functioning and Avoiding Collapse During Recovery* (1989). Videocassettes available through Healing Hearts (1989) (see Resources).

Chapter 4

Physical, Sexual, and Emotional Abuse of Children: Brainwashing and Programming

Dream: April 11, 1985

I was at the kitchen table eating dinner with my family. Everyone was talking and laughing, and I kept trying to say something. Their conversation became louder, drowning out my voice. Nobody looked at me. Nobody acknowledged that I had said something. I felt like I was in a glass cage. I could see out, but no one could see in. The feelings of isolation were unbearable. I walked over to my mother and started pulling on her sleeve. "Mom, Mom, listen to me!" I pleaded. She continued to laugh with the others, without so much as her head turning toward me. I looked up at my entire family. "Listen to me!" I screamed. "Why won't you listen to me?" Still, they didn't look at me. I felt like I was invisible. Anger burned inside of me. The frustration made every cell in my body turn to fire. I hated them, but there was nothing I could do to make them acknowledge my existence.

I reached for a hammer and smashed my arm. "Look at this!" I said. "Do you see this?" Still no one noticed. I became crazed with my fury to hurt myself. I was mocking just how little they cared. "Look at this!" I said, and I started rubbing my body on the carpet as hard as I could to give it rug burn. I felt nothing. My body didn't exist. All I wanted to do was hurt my family, and my body was the tool I could use to show just what they had done to me. I wanted to make people see the pain. I wanted to mock the games of silence I never had control over. Still nobody noticed.

There was a knock at the door. I got up and answered it. It was my best friend, Kristin. She looked at me with horror, "Oh, my God," she said. "What have you done?" For the first time, I looked down at my body and noticed the torn and mangled flesh. I felt confused and numb. I had never noticed the physical damage. "We've got to call the ambulance," she said. I was quiet. I didn't know what to do anymore.

The ambulance came, and they hooked me up to an I.V. and a life-support system. The medic looked down at me and said, "You know you may die." I looked over my body and saw the bruised limbs and the tired bones. I felt overwhelmed with grief. My body had paid the price for all the pain I could never express in words. I realized that the most important relationship in my life is the relationship I have with myself. Who was my family, anyway? Who were any of those people who ignored me? My body was going to die. I was going to die. What had I done to deserve any of this?

I had punished me because I could never punish anyone else. I always vented my frustration on me because no one else could acknowledge the all-penetrating injustices perpetrated against me. In that final instance, I saw it. I saw that no matter what happens, that no matter what anyone ever says or does to me, it will never be worth losing me. And I felt it. I truly felt it. Me—without anyone's opinions or ideas of what I was. Just me. I looked at my body, and I truly remembered. I knew I had to keep living. I had found my reason to survive.

Although many different groups engage in ritual abuse, the abuse has many common characteristics. Sexual abuse, animal and human sacrifice, and physical torture are common themes. Many groups also profit financially from child pornography and child prostitution. Most victims of ritual abuse report being drugged during the abuse. Due to the effects of the drugs, many of the ritual abuse memories may have a distant, foggy quality, as survivors remember the abuse in therapy. Tables 4.1 and 4.2 list the types of abuse perpetrated against ritual abuse survivors in our study.

Table 4.1   The Forms of Abuse Perpetrated Against Ritual Abuse Survivors

Molestation or intercourse	100%
Forced participation in group sex with adults	96%
Torture of you	94%
Witnessing or forced participation in animal sacrifice	90%
Witnessing or forced participation in human sacrifice	88%
Sodomy	88%
Drugged during the abuse	88%
Witnessing or forced participation in cannibalism	82%
Forced to torture others	75%
Child prostitution	52%
Child pornography	52%
Forced to breed children who were later sacrificed	36%

Table 4.2   Other Forms of Abuse Mentioned by Ritual Abuse Survivors

Mental programming	21%
Bestiality	17%
Use of electric shock for torture	13%
Witnessing/forced participation in dismemberment/mutilation of bodies	12%
Being hung upside down	10%
Forced to kidnap children from playgrounds	8%
Hypnotism	8%
Pets killed	4%
Psychic surgery	4%
Being rented out to other cults	4%

HUMAN AND ANIMAL SACRIFICE

Violent cult rituals often involve the sacrificial killing of animals or
humans. One survivor recalls in detail the killings she witnessed
during the rituals.

> In all, I believe I witnessed the murders of six people as
> part of the rituals. They were: a baby who was dismembered
> and killed with an ax, a baby who was stabbed to death by
> my mother, a baby who was stabbed by a man, a young
> pregnant woman who was stabbed in the stomach (to kill the
> fetus also), a mentally retarded or schizophrenic man who
> was given a lethal injection, and a man who was stabbed to
> death. There may have been others, but these are the only
> ones I have distinct memories of...
>
> When people or animals were stabbed to death, their
> blood was caught in a gold bowl, and then everyone drank
> some of it. Parts of the bodies, such as hearts and organs,
> were also eaten.

Consumption of blood and flesh, performed in a communion-
like fashion, is usually an integral part of ritual sacrifice. Rituals
sometimes involve the killing of children and adults, and the acts
are not necessarily carried out in the name of Satan. One survivor
describes a ritual similar to the one noted above, where the purpose
of the ritual was to seek purification from God:

> In 1952 or 1953, at the age of eight or nine, I witnessed
> the ritual sexual abuse and murder of children in a Christian
> "healing church" within an hour's drive or so of my home in
> Maryland.
>
> The church was an ornate mausoleum, with stained glass
> windows high on the walls and with crypts for the storage of
> embalmed bodies. Wooden pews faced a long, stage-like
> altar. The pulpit stood to the worshipers' right...
>
> According to the preacher, the Day of Judgment was near
> at hand (as evidenced by the practice of air raids, bomb
> shelters, and city evacuation plans of the Cold War), so the
> salvation of souls was urgent. He said the old people before

him had already grown wise in the work of the Lord; their survival as exemplars of the faith was essential. In order that those men might continue the work of the Lord, he said sanctified children "had offered their own vitality in Christian sacrifice." These little girls, lined up on the altar, were "saints" voluntarily surrendering their lives that their elders might live to spread the Gospel among those yet unsaved before the Day of Judgment. The men had only to "embrace" the pure children (that is, copulate with them) to receive a share of their vitality. During the "communion" rituals at the church, the girls, four to ten years old, thus discharged their "life force" to the men over a period of several weeks until they were completely emptied (that is, dead).

Violent cults use a variety of justifications for these human and animal sacrifices. Some groups state that human sacrifice is no different than the animal sacrifices of the past. They note that the God of the Old Testament demanded animal sacrifices in his name. In their belief system, human beings are nothing more than complex animals, and they have no more right to life than any other creature on the earth. If the God of the Old Testament demanded animal sacrifice, they say, why is the sacrifice of a larger animal, a human, more of a sin than the sacrifice of a smaller animal, such as a lamb?

Some groups state that the ritual context is the only justified place for killings. In life, in order for anything to survive, something must die. Be it an animal or a plant, something must be killed. This is the law of nature, the food chain, the act of eating. Some groups may claim that the sacrifice of animals or humans in rituals brings them closer to understanding the natural order of life, which naturally encompasses death. They view the sacrifices as a way to directly confront this natural cycle of life and death in a systematic, structured fashion. By killing in a ritual, as opposed to random killing for food or during war, the group claims to connect the act to something higher than themselves. To a group based on this philosophy, the human or animal sacrifice is just that, a sacrifice. One creature dies to regenerate the life of all the rest. In such a belief system, the death of the sacrifice results in greater wisdom for all people who witness the death of the victim.

No matter what philosophical justification is used for the "sacrifice," children always see the act as a cold-hearted murder. Children who watch people or animals killed are terrified as they watch the creature die. It is one thing to eat a salad; it is another thing to watch creatures suffer, knowing that you could ease their pain. If the adults in the groups connect to the feelings of the helpless, desperate child, they realize that no justification stops the intense pain, loneliness, and fear.

CHILD ABUSE

Adults who sexually, physically, or emotionally violate children attempt to rationalize their behavior in order to stop their own guilt. Some adults claim that physical child abuse is "discipline." The adults believe they have a right to physically assault children if the assault is justified by some principle, such as, "You asked for the beating by talking back." In the case of ritual abuse, secrecy maintains the smooth operation of the group. If the child tells someone about the ritual abuse, the child is disciplined, that is, punished with torture. For example, the abuser might insert needles into the child's genitals, all the while telling her she is evil. Other torture might include stretching, electrical shock, prolonged confinement with body parts or insects, or being hung upside down, while verbally instilling the same lesson.

Some adults in cults justify their violent behavior by telling themselves they are preparing their victims for the difficult struggles of life. No matter what justification is used for the ritual abuse, the violence is always about the exploitation of helpless victims. When adults steal children's rights of physical and emotional safety, the violating acts are about the abusers' own pain. They are capable of hurting children without remorse because of their own emotional isolation from other human beings.

Some cults abuse children in order to make the children "stronger" than other people, to create a "superior" breed of people who can withstand any degree of pain. Sometimes the abused children are nothing more than objects used for magical purposes during rituals. Many magical teachings are based on the belief that people reach higher levels of spiritual awareness through pain and suffering. Sometimes magicians inflict the pain on themselves, and sometimes on innocent victims. Children in these situations become nothing more than another article—like a robe, altar, or candle—used during the ritual. They are treated as inanimate objects. Children are also used by their abusers to satisfy the abusers' sadistic fantasies.

The sexual, physical, and emotional assaults on the children in all ritual abuse contexts appear to have specific, unspoken functions. Violent cults want to control their victims. Most often, the goal of the ritual abuse is indoctrination. Children abused in these cults learn that their bodies are not their own and that anyone can touch them or do whatever they like. Children learn they are neither physically, sexually, nor emotionally safe. They must obey those around them or risk being attacked.

The abuse is intended to make the children feel helpless and ashamed. The more helpless and hopeless the children feel, the easier they are to control. A great deal of the ritual abuse is also designed to make the children feel responsible for things they had no choice about. The cults deliberately set up scenes where a child is forced to commit or witness a violent act, only for the group to turn on the child. Cult members tell her that what happened was her fault, because she is "evil" or "bad." The child learns that she cannot control what goes on around her. She learns that no matter what, she will always be the one at fault. On a deep, feeling, child level, ritual abuse survivors are taught they are responsible for every bad thing that happens around them, and that no matter what, they can't change any of it. A survivor describes an example of this brainwashing during a lynching:

> At one point, [my father] kicked me and knocked me down. He said to me, "That nigger fucked you, and that's why we had to cut his balls off and string him up. He fucked you because you asked for it, showing off your little tits and all that, you little whore. You helped us cut him up and string him up. So, for the rest of your life, all the niggers of the world will be coming after you to kill you, and you will have to let them do anything they want."

None of what he said was actually true. I don't believe I was ever abused by a black man, and I certainly did not participate in the torture and lynching of this man.

Many cults pervert or misuse Christian teachings in an attempt to make the child feel guilty and ashamed. A survivor gives this example:

> On specific holidays throughout the year, the cult would engage in rituals which mock or oppose Christianity. At Christmas, rather than baby Jesus being born, he was tortured, sexually abused, and murdered by "Mother Mary," Joseph, and the Three Wise Men. Also they told me after that ritual: "Jesus died for your sins. You are bad. You should have died. It is blasphemy what you did. You are bad. He died because of *your* sins. You should be punished."

Most survivors noted that eventually they were forced to participate in the violence. One survivor stated:

> On at least one occasion, I was forced to participate in a murder . . . I knew they were going to kill him, and some adult (I don't know who) came up to me and put my hand around the sharp knife's handle and this person closed his or her hand around mine, and together we cut off the man's penis. Then he was stabbed to death by the adult. They told me I had taken his "manhood" and that because of that, I would have to take on the role of a male, and that I could never enjoy being a girl or a woman.

Cults are able to cut children off from their own sense of what feels right and what feels wrong by forcing them to participate in violent acts. Many survivors recall being forced to hurt and kill the things they love. Some survivors recall being forced to kill their pets. For a child living in such an isolated environment, being forced to kill a pet may be like killing her only friend in the world. By making the child betray the things she loves, the cult is able to force her to rely solely on the group for any emotional nurturing.

PROGRAMMING

Many groups deliberately program ideas and beliefs into their victims during overwhelmingly painful torture sessions. For example, while needles are inserted in her vagina, a girl might be told she is filled with poison that infects anyone she loves. Survivors are usually programmed with specific information about how to behave outside the cults. While being tortured, they are told to never talk about the abuse. They are told how to act and who to have as friends.

Torture used during programming usually takes the form of electrical shock, stretching, or poking with needles—methods that do not leave marks. One survivor remembers:

> There was a doctor present at each one of the rituals who seemed to have a special high-ranking position. The doctor advised the people who were torturing the children on just what to do, and what not to do, to leave any marks. And after the ceremony was over, he treated some of the injuries and explained to the parents what they could say to explain away the injuries, in case school officials or anyone else asked.

In the case of children abused by their parents, if the torture ever caused enough physical damage for someone to suspect abuse, parents might have kept the child at home "with the flu."

Hypnosis is also used to enhance the effects of programming. Hypnosis and torture are used to gain control of every aspect of victims' lives. As ritually abused children grow up, hypnosis and torture are used to program where to go to school, what to do as a job, and even who to marry.

Programming also involves teaching children that they are somehow superior to others. This common brainwashing tactic alienates the children from any sense of belonging with other "ordinary" human beings. This sense of "specialness" is the only positive feeling children raised in cults are allowed to feel. The children learn to identify this feeling with belonging to the cult. The cults use this ploy of "specialness" to keep the children bonded to the group. One survivor recalls:

The leader soon learned he could make us do or believe anything he wanted. On one end of the spectrum, he told us we were Kali, goddess of destruction, and we would do unspeakable acts for him. On the other end, he would use drugs, hypnosis, and torture to make us not reveal anything about the cult.

Triggers

Victims are programmed under torture to respond to specific triggers, such as certain colors or words. Using the trigger stimulus, the cults are able to contact the personalities who were born during the torture. After being triggered, survivors forget what they did while they were in their other personality. The groups use trigger words or symbols to bring survivors to meetings or rituals against their will.

For example, a survivor who wants to break free of the cult might do everything in her power to get away from her abusers, only to receive a phone call from them in the middle of the night. When she answers the phone, she hears bells and a voice that whispers, "Come." The word "come" is a trigger word she learned during torture. The message she learned about the trigger was that when she hears the word "come," she needs to go to a ritual or else they will find her and torture her again. When the survivor hears the trigger, she immediately switches personalities and complies with the wishes of her abusers. The next morning the survivor wakes up completely unaware that she received the phone call or went to a ritual.

To summarize, programming is about control. It is about brainwashing the child into becoming a member of the group. Most of the programming is designed to protect the group's secrecy. The silence of all members is an essential priority of all cults that ritually abuse children.

Because it is done so consistently during such traumatic situations, programming seems to have mechanical effects on survivors. Without even realizing it, survivors respond to triggers and programming they learned during their childhood. Programming has an even greater effect on survivors when brainwashing is intertwined with the survivors' true feelings. Separating their true feelings and fears from programming helps survivors break the hold the brain-washing has on them. The following are examples of typical cult programming and how it taps into the real feelings of survivors.

Suicide

Many abusers program survivors under torture to commit suicide if they ever remember or tell of the ritual abuse. This is the easiest way for cults to get rid of members who do not comply with the rules of silence. A suicide makes the survivor look like the problem and discredits the claims of abuse.

Feeling suicidal is a very common experience for ritual abuse survivors. Survivors of ritual abuse experience excruciatingly high levels of pain. Survivors raised in cults, if they choose to leave, often have to cut ties with old friends and family members. They constantly have to keep their eyes open for people who may attempt to pull them back into a cult. The lives of ritual abuse survivors trying to break free are filled with fear and dread at the possibility of having to face the abusers. They are plagued with loneliness and the feeling that they don't belong anywhere.

Survivors who are still being ritually abused today are faced with the greatest feelings of hopelessness. They feel utterly helpless, like animals trapped in locked cages. These survivors see no escape from their lives of suffering. To these people, suicide appears to be the easiest and quickest solution.

Suicidal feelings also surface through the memory process. As survivors begin to remember the abuse, they experience the same feelings as when the abuse was happening. This is a natural part of the memory process; however, without an understanding of the pain, the survivor may believe the suffering will last forever. The physical and emotional pain is so intense that the survivor may want to die. It seems she can numb the pain by killing herself or hurting her body. Suicidal feelings are very common among people abused in cults. They let the survivor know in the deepest manner possible, "I wanted more than this." It is important for all survivors to remember that it is a mistake to act on these suicidal feelings. There is hope for change today.

Self-Mutilation

Some violent cults teach survivors to internalize their "punishment" for going against the teachings of the group. As punishment, survivors are programmed to cut themselves or to hurt themselves if they ever tell people about cult activities. Again, survivors are usually taught this lesson during torture sessions. They are told trigger words to make them hurt themselves at the command of their abusers and told to self-mutilate if they ever go against the group.

Survivors who tell about the abuse are faced with the justified fear of not being believed. Many survivors have been victimized when they told of the ritual abuse. Survivors have been told they were possessed, blamed for the abuse, and not believed. The injustices perpetrated against survivors by the cult and by society are so great that some survivors feel they have only one way to express their anger and frustration. The only person's behavior they can control is their own, so they turn their frustration and anger inward and they cut their own bodies. They turn on themselves because other people do not hear their pain or accept the truth of what they say.

For many survivors, telling about the abuse also leads to validation of the memories, which causes more pain. When survivors accept that their memories are true, they must grieve for everything they have lost. Often they become plagued with self-destructive impulses because they are so furious and hurt by the past they cannot change.

Acting on self-mutilating impulses causes survivors more pain in the long run. When survivors are able to find a safe environment, they are able to ride out the pain of the memories with support. They are then free to scream about the injustices committed against them. They grieve their losses. In the end, they live in their own personal truth. They regain their lives.

Kill the Person You Tell

Some violent cults also protect their secrets by programming survivors to kill the people they tell about the abuse. Once again, people label the survivors as insane and invalidate the memories of ritual abuse.

This programming is usually taught during torture sessions. Or the child might be put into a situation where she is allowed to get close to a cult member. When she tells the cult member about abuse perpetrated against her, the member turns on her and aligns with the abusers. She feels like killing this individual, and the abusers may use this rage from the trauma to control the child. They may tell her that all people that she tells about the abuse will eventually betray her, and she is best off to kill them soon after she discloses.

This programming to kill taps into the survivor's valid desire to protect herself. If someone breaks into her house and attacks her, then she has the right to use whatever violence necessary to stop the attack. All people have this right to self-defense. But survivors of ritual abuse were never allowed to defend themselves in the cult context. These natural feelings for self-protection have been twisted by the cults into a blind rage that the cults control. The survivors never received any genuine relief for their rage because their feelings could never be expressed to the people who violated and controlled their every move. Cults use this blind rage to force survivors to commit acts of violence.

Kill Someone You Love

Survivors are also programmed to kill the people they love. By teaching survivors to betray their own most intimate relationships, the cult is able to destroy the survivors' connections to other people. Children abused in violent cults often bond with one another, and the cults use these relationships time and time again to hurt the survivors. They force close friends to betray and humiliate each other. Eventually, the children are so confused about love and their feelings that killing people they are fond of seems easier than having to betray them or be betrayed by them at the next ritual.

This programming taps into survivors' own uncomfortable feelings about being vulnerable: When they were vulnerable in the past, they were betrayed. These violent cults teach children that they are unlovable. They tell them that no one will ever care about them. This type of emotional cruelty makes the children ache so badly for love that when they finally feel love inside and reach out to someone, they are paralyzed with fear that the love might not be returned. Their entire sense of worth—in proving that the cults are wrong—lies in the hands of the beloved. This degree of vulnerability is uncomfortable, if not unbearable. By killing the loved one, survivors destroy their chance to feel the pleasure of being loved, but they are able to cease the discomfort of not knowing if the love is returned. It sometimes seems easier to stay numb than to open up and possibly have your feelings rejected.

Love/Hate Relationships Between Cult Members

Children raised together in violent cults develop powerful bonds, similar to the bonds that develop between war veterans. Cults use these close relationships to keep survivors bonded to the group. Cults also use these relationships to teach survivors that they will never be able to trust or love anyone without feeling hurt and betrayed.

Cults deliberately set up scenes where friends betray each other. For example, a cult might force children who are close friends to beat and torture each other, and then convince the injured child that his friend wanted to do these cruel things. When the children grow up, they learn to enjoy betraying the people they love, much in the same way that they learn to hurt themselves to survive the pain. Initially, neither child had control of the violent scenes. They were both trapped in a situation that neither of them could change. They learned to do as they were told, even if it meant betraying their strongest feelings to treat their loved one with kindness.

As the children grow older, they feel intense love and intense hatred for the people they are bonded to in the cult. For many survivors, not only is the beloved the person who made them feel loved and special, but the beloved is also the one who tore their heart to shreds when he complied with the wishes of the cult to betray them. These betrayed survivors carry the hidden shame and remorse for all the times they were forced to betray the loved one as well. The survivors end up feeling as if their love is tainted and dangerous.

But love is not what caused the betrayal. The reality is that the children were trapped. Love gave the children their few fleeting glimpses of security and pleasure. It was the cult that betrayed the children. It was the cult that taught them love is about pain.

If You Ever Tell, We Will Kill You

Many violent cults threaten survivors and harass them in an attempt to bring them back under the influence of the group. Cults promise to kill any survivor who tells of the ritual abuse. Through experience, survivors know that these cults are capable of killing. Despite these threats, cults usually do not seem to act on their warnings. The first priority in violent cults is to maintain intense secrecy. Cults are more interested in keeping their existence secret than in killing a member who may be attempting to leave the group. From their perspective, their energy is probably better spent pursuing survivors who are trying to get out to manipulate them to return, rather than acting on their threats to kill survivors.

People who attempt to leave the cult often face such overwhelming denial and revictimization that they eventually give up the struggle to find a better life. The fact that most people do not believe ritual abuse exists adds to the power cults have over their victims. As a result, many survivors never find the help they need to break free. It is very difficult for survivors to get out, and the groups are able to move in and pull survivors back in at their weakest moments.

We Will Kill the People You Love

Many violent cults threaten to kill the people survivors love, but usually do not act on this threat. Again, acting on it might be a mistake. If the loved one of a survivor is a noncult member, killing the nonmember would validate the survivor's memories of the ritual abuse. Moreover, killing the friend would leave the cult vulnerable to attack from noncult people who may have cared about the murder victim. This would break the first rule of secrecy. After examining their priorities, they may decide that keeping any single member is not worth jeopardizing the existence of the entire group.

It is also not in the cult's best interest to kill a loved one who is a cult member. Cults spend a great deal of time programming and raising each survivor to hold a specific role within the group. Killing one member because they are about to lose another would potentially result in losing them both. They know that if they acted on the threat to kill this individual, the survivor trying to get out would lose a strong tie to the cult. In fact, the survivor would probably hate the group even more. Therefore, it seems to be a more effective tactic for the cult to keep the loved one alive while continuing with the threats.

If You Leave, We Will Torture the Cult Member You Love

Many violent cults threaten to harm someone the survivor knows is a cult member. The cults have access to these people for torture or physical deprivation. The bonds between cult members are the most powerful weapons the cults use to make survivors comply with their wishes. Threatening to harm a loved one in the cult is enough to keep most survivors from leaving. Cults are very capable of carrying out these threats. Often close friends and family members are also members of the group, and risking their safety may not seem worth a failed attempt to leave the group.

Unfortunately, even if the survivor stays in the cult, this loved one will still be hurt and so will she. By leaving the group, the survivor gives a chance for others to follow. As long as people remain cult members, they remain unable to protect themselves or the people they love from the physical and mental cruelties of the group. The best way to protect loved ones is for survivors to get out themselves and show by example that it is possible to have a new way of life free of control by others.

We Are Magic

Violent cults want children to believe they are all-powerful. They try to convince children that they have magical powers. Often they tell the children that they can read their minds and send evil spirits after them if they misbehave or betray them. Survivors sometimes feel the presence of alter personalities who believe they were possessed. The sensation is actually a memory of how each survivor felt at a certain point during the ritual abuse experience. It is not the wrath of spirits that cults control. The acts committed against survivors, the horrible feelings that they must have felt, combined with the cult framing the emotional experience of the children as "evil spirits controlling their bodies," all lead survivors to explain this particular sensation of loss of body control as a possession. The evil spirit is really the final eruption of the repressed emotional energy that the survivor can no longer control.

Abusers pretend to have magical powers to intimidate children into compliance. They use these lies to make children feel powerless. Sometimes, as survivors remember the abuse, coincidentally at the same time something bad happens to them—they may get in a car accident or get cancer, for example. These natural occurrences, which happen to ritual abuse survivors and non-ritual abuse survivors alike, are sometimes mistaken as proof by survivors and their advocates that the cults in fact have magical powers. This interpretation of survivors' traumatic experiences is extremely revictimizing. Survivors of ritual abuse have a right to get sick and face tragedy in the same way that all people face their painful life experiences. They have a right to face life tragedies without feeling "cursed" because of their ritual abuse experience.

You Are Crazy . . . It's Only a Dream

What violent cults do to children makes them feel the craziness of never knowing what is real. Often they tell children that the ritual abuse is only a dream, a very, very bad dream. They tell children that kids actually enjoy being sexually and physically abused. They make the children thank them after they have been beaten. They teach children never to trust their own perceptions of reality, by lying to them about what is happening. The overwhelming feelings children experience during the abuse exacerbate the feeling of being out of control and "crazy."

As the memories surface in later life, it is very confusing for survivors to understand why they never remembered any of the abuse until that moment. They may feel crazy, but they also feel a strong sense of familiarity, which lets them know they are not making any of it up. Survivors of ritual abuse are often accused by others of being crazy. With the statement "You are crazy," people are able to completely discount and minimize a person's feelings, thoughts, and behavior. "Oh, that person is just crazy. No one can believe what he says." The survivor who is told that she is crazy is told that her reality is not the truth. When a person's reality is denied, she may feel crazy, but that is very different from actually being psychotic.

You Are Evil ... You Belong with Us

Many groups teach children that they are evil and belong only with the cult group. They tell children that people outside the group see their "defective, evil cores." They claim that whenever anything bad happens to the children, it's because people finally see the blackness inside their souls. These children learn that whenever they are victimized by others, they have asked for the attack in some way. They learn that there is something innately wrong with them that will never change.

"No one else will ever want you," the cults tell the children. Abused children believe these lies because they are plagued with self-loathing for what they were forced to do. Initially, before the children are able to dissociate from the feelings, the children feel excruciatingly painful self-resentment, guilt, and self-hate. They know the things they were forced to do were "bad," and they identify this badness with themselves. The ritual abuse sets these children apart from people who were not raised in cults. If the children accept that they are bad, then they can belong somewhere—with the cult—and not be alone. Sometimes their only hope for acceptance or love appears to be with other cult members.

You Can Never Make Mistakes

Many violent cults program children to perform violent and non-violent acts during rituals. Children who make mistakes are severely reprimanded. Under the guise of discipline, cults intimidate children into not thinking about what the cults are forcing them to do. All the children worry about during the ritual is whether they are doing the act "right."

This type of intensive structure cuts children off from their own internal sense of right and wrong. By dictating the children's actions, and then by threatening the children with violence if they don't comply, the cult is able to control the children's thoughts during the abuse. For example, take a child who is slowly being trained to hold a specific role in the ritual. Each time the child makes a mistake, the child is tortured. Soon, the child is only aware of whether she is acting in a way that will keep her from being hurt. This keeps her from reflecting upon her own feelings and thoughts about what is happening during the ritual.

In some violent cults, making a mistake is followed by extreme torture. During the torture, children ask themselves, "Why are they hurting me? Why?" The simplistic answer in the child's mind is, "Because they don't like me." For a child, that is the worst pain of all. Wanting to be perfect is another way of saying I just want to be liked.

We Are Your Family

Survivors are taught that the only life worth living is a life as a member of the cult. Cults often refer to themselves as family even if they are not blood relatives. They try to make children feel loyal and dedicated to the group in the way that most people feel dedicated to their biological families. Under the guise of "parenting," the cult determines for the children their present and future behavior.

Survivors who go against the wishes of the cult sometimes feel like failures for betraying "their family." If survivors choose a life other than the one the cult has planned for them, sometimes they become plagued with thoughts like, "I am a failure . . . I will never amount to anything." These messages are placed in the survivors' minds during torture sessions and throughout the abuse to keep them from ever having enough self-esteem to go against the desires of the group.

It's Too Late . . . There's Nothing You Can Do

Many violent cults tell children that there is no hope and no way out. Abusers constantly relay this message to children during torture sessions and reiterate it when the children are feeling hopeless. For example, an abuser might put a child's pet on an altar and kill it, after the child has tried desperately to make the abuser stop. Then the abuser laughs at the sobbing child and says, "It's over. It's too late. There is no way out."

In the past, in many ways, the abusers were right. It was too late. Less than ten years ago, if survivors told of the ritual abuse, they were thrown in mental hospitals and diagnosed as paranoid schizophrenics. Today, however, this attitude is changing. Survivors can remember the ritual abuse, and their own current entrapment and find adequate help. They can reach out for help and be heard.

Survivors who believe there is no escape from the pain feel completely helpless. As children, they couldn't stop the abuse, no matter how loudly they cried or screamed. As adults, they may have watched their own children being tortured or killed, unable to stop what was happening. The cults teach their members that they have no control of what happens around them, that their behavior has no effect on their environment. Survivors learn that no matter what they do, they are doomed to receive more pain. This learned helplessness may prevent survivors from being able to leave the group as adults.

You're a Fool

Ritual abusers hurt the people, animals, and toys that the children love. Children who try to protect the things they love, or who act on their feelings to help and give to others, are ridiculed and mocked. For example, the abusers may deliberately set up a situation in which the child believes one of the cult members is going to protect her and love her. The child loves the savior adult and takes action to protect the adult from harm. When the child tries to protect the adult, the adult turns on the child and start to laugh at her. The adult says he likes to be hurt, and that the child is a fool to try to protect him. The child feels confused and betrayed. The message she receives is that she is a fool if she ever tries to help another person. They teach a memorable lesson: that just like her, her love or help is tainted and dirty.

Cults always make fun of the positive expression of love. People are mocked when they express their love for other cult members, and they are taught that no one in the cult is capable of loving another human being. They also don't believe that anyone could honestly love a member of the cult, because they see their own internalized shame and disgust in other people. They believe they are all too "evil" to be loved. Love, however, is what allows cult members the ability to fight the pain and programming of the cult. Making survivors feel like fools when they love other people keeps survivors from feeling the strength that comes from the power of love. If they never feel the strength that is found in love—in the ability to feel—then they will have difficulty breaking free of the cult.

No One Will Ever Love You

The cults tell the children that they will never be loved by anyone, that they are tainted and messed up inside, and that anyone who gets close to them will see their "dirtiness." For example, as a child complies with the wishes of his abusers and hurts a helpless creature, an abuser might turn to a friend of the child's and say, "Look at him! Look at him!" meaning, look at how "evil" and "disgusting" your friend has become. This causes the child who complied with the abusers to feel that his close friend has now seen his "dirty, evil core."

The cults tell the children these lies in order to bond them to the group. People who feel they will never be loved experience life as utterly and completely meaningless. This gives the cults the opportunity to control every aspect of the victim's life. If the victims no longer care what happens, then the cults can make them do whatever they want.

Survivors of ritual abuse feel this ache for love, which they often identify as the reality that they have never been loved. It is a painful and devastating thought. However, there may be times when people feel angry at us or not even care whether we live or die, but everyone has been loved, if at least for a moment.

The pain identified by survivors as the reality that they were "never loved" is a deep realization of the isolated lives they had to endure because of the ritual abuse. Each survivor knows there are places deep inside that no one—except for someone else who has been abused in a cult—could understand. And many times those who have also been ritually abused are drowning in their own pain and are unable to provide her with the support she needs. The survivor needs a nurturing love that she believes she will never find.

This deep knowledge that her needs may never be met fits with the cult's message that "No one will ever love you!" because that may be how it feels to not have your needs met.

You Are So Special

Children in many violent cults are programmed to feel special and superior to other human beings. They are given specific roles within the group that are most suited to their personalities. These children often are told that they are a goddess, Jesus, or some other important figure. For example, at a ritual a little girl may be dressed up in a fancy costume and told she is a goddess who has a message for the world. She is told that ordinary human beings will never understand her. This form of brainwashing is a deep and devastating betrayal of a child's need to feel loved. It keeps the child from ever feeling connected to other human beings.

Young children naturally feel special. Children love to fantasize that they are the queen or king of the land. This natural feeling of specialness is not the type of specialness we think of as adults, but is based on a deep and powerful love for oneself. It is not about arrogance and power. It is about wanting to be the most loved and important person in the world, the one who gets all the good attention. Manipulating this feeling of specialness betrays the child's love for herself and her desire to be loved by others.

It feels good to be told you are special. When you are truly loved by someone, you are the most special, the most loved person in the loved one's life. The programming of being "special" taps into this need to receive special love and recognition from another person. But to the child's detriment, this programming is designed to make the child feel superior and different from other people rather than cherished and wanted.

To add to the confusion, children who are programmed to believe that they are special are continually reminded as adults that they are mere members of the group and "no better than anyone else." If an adult member talks about feeling special, others look down on him. It is taboo in the cults to toot your own horn. Many violent cults don't want adult members to feel any self-love or to express any positive feelings toward themselves. If individual members believed they were special and powerful, they might have enough strength to go against the group and break free. Cults do not want their members to feel empowered unless the feelings are controlled and tamed by the cult belief system.

Each member is torn by a sense of specialness that contradicts their deep feelings of being "evil" and "unlovable." When anyone reminds them of this contradiction by sharing their own feelings of specialness, other members immediately want the person to be silenced.

You Can Save the World

Many violent cults tell their members they can save the world. During a ritual, for example, the abusers might set up a scene where a small child is allowed to rescue an animal that is about to be killed. The abusers then tell her there are many animals suffering in the world that all need her help. They ask her, "What would you do to save all the animals?" They tell her that if she figures out how to do it, they will help her. They make her feel that saving an individual is not important. It is the entire world that must be changed, and she has the power to do it.

If members believe that they can someday change everything that has ever caused them pain, they do not feel the pain of their losses. This programming saves individuals from killing themselves when they do feel hopeless and trapped in the cult; it restores the feeling of individual control and convinces them they can make changes. However, this programming also makes them believe that they are not only responsible for their own happiness, but also for the happiness of the entire world. There is no way that any one single person can change the entire world. This dream of saving the world is like a soothing narcotic hope, but in reality it prevents people from taking care of themselves.

Abusers use this programming time and time again to manipulate survivors. If survivors use this fantasy to suppress their hard-felt grief, they will inevitably feel a desperate need to protect the fantasy of saving the world—even if it means sacrificing their own lives.

Hatred for the World

Cults control children by isolating them from the larger society. They make children feel like they belong to an elite group that will someday have control of the entire world. They teach them that the cult is right, and that everyone else in the world is wrong. They view noncult people as weak and inferior. Their belief systems are based on a deep hatred for all people who have never been members of the cult.

Most survivors of ritual abuse harbor some resentment for the larger society that did not protect them. The cults use this justified resentment for society to bond its members to the group. They make survivors feel completely isolated and alienated from the larger society. They teach survivors that there is no place to turn for help. Just ten years ago, survivors did not have a place to turn. Today, things are changing. Survivors who persistently search for adequate help find it.

If They Find Out, They Will Throw You in Jail!

Many violent cults are able to silence children by making them feel responsible for what happens in the cult. Children are told that if others knew what they had done in the cult, then people would lock them in a cage. Sometimes cults even act out scenarios in rituals where they place children in cages to show them what jail feels like. The children are terrified by these threats because they know bad people go to jail, and they know they were forced to do very bad things in the cult. The children become terrified of the law and of the larger society because they think everyone would hate them and punish them if they found out what they had done in the rituals. At the same time, they feel a bitter hatred and resentment for the "law." For children raised in cults, the laws of the country they live in some-times seem like hypocritical laws that protect everyone but them.

When ritually abused children are unable to escape from their abusers, they are afraid to remember current ritual abuse memories for fear that they might be put in jail. Many adult ritual abuse survivors who are stuck in cults today are afraid to try to get out because of this threat. In some ways, the cults are right. Unfortunately, in a court of law, it is very difficult for adult ritual abuse survivors charged with ritual abuse to prove they were brainwashed from childhood to commit the acts. Even if the adults were tortured from when they were babies never to seek help or tell of the abuse, it is not regarded as an excuse. It is not an excuse that most of them never had a choice to become anything other than a "willing" member of the group. As a result, these survivors once again feel horribly betrayed by the system.

If You Tell, They'll Lock You Up in a Mental Hospital!

Unfortunately, this threat sometimes comes true. It is not uncommon for survivors to end up in psychiatric hospitals as they remember the abuse. Some survivors choose to be hospitalized; other survivors are hospitalized against their will by their therapists because of suicidal feelings or acts.

In the hospitals, survivors are often drugged and treated with grave disrespect. Few psychiatric hospitals are based on the philosophy of empowering the patient. Most hospitals frame patients as "mentally ill" or "unhealthy" as a result of the abuse. They do not address ritual abuse survivors as people who were severely traumatized as children. Even some of the hospitals specifically for people with dissociative disorders revictimize survivors. In these hospitals, the staff treat the "mental illness" of MPD as opposed to providing a supportive, nurturing environment for the survivors in which they are able to express the truth of their deep emotional pain in an empowering manner.

Trauma centers, as opposed to psychiatric hospitals, appear to have a more empowering philosophy regarding the role of dissociation in the abuse. Trauma centers are aware that the abuse, not the multiple personalities, is what causes survivors' pain. Enlightened trauma centers treat the personalities as the guardians of the truth. Unfortunately, survivors have reported revictimization even in trauma centers.

Survivors must be cautious as they remember the abuse. They need to find therapists who will respect their feelings about hospitalization. They need to remember that therapists cannot legally put their clients in mental hospitals unless they believe the clients are going to act on feelings to cause harm to themselves or others. In the case of therapy for ritual abuse survivors, the threat of hospitalization should not stop survivors from talking about homicidal or suicidal thoughts or feelings. These feelings are a common part of remembering ritual abuse, and talking about violent feelings need not be an indication that survivors intend to act on the feelings.

Survivors must learn early in the process of remembering, through cooperation and communication in the multiple system, to keep their personalities from putting the entire system in situations where they might legally require hospitalization in a revictimizing facility. Personalities can talk about the suicidal or homicidal feelings, but acting on the feelings is hurtful to the system as a whole. The personalities must work together to keep them all as safe as possible.

People Will Think You Are a Child Molester

If survivors can identify with a child and feel a child's pain, then they are unable to participate in the rituals. Many violent cults teach all members to be afraid of children because they want the survivors to hate children, to resent children. This programming is one of the most devastating forms of programming for survivors because the pain of being forced to abuse children is perhaps the greatest pain of all. For survivors, it is taking part in what led them to their own destruction.

In the cult environment, survivors do not have a choice when they are forced to molest another child. They commit these acts against their will, then they hate themselves and wish there was a punishment great enough to make the guilt stop. Many violent cults tell all their members, children and adults, that if they are seen around children, people will believe they are molesting children outside of the cult. This programming taps into the survivors' shame from the ritual abuse. The only way some survivors are able to deal with the painful thoughts is to avoid children altogether.

Since survivors saw children being abused as they were growing up, sometimes they feel plagued with thoughts of molestation and child abuse whenever they are around children. Survivors think there is something innately wrong with them to make them think such thoughts. But it should be no surprise that children would remind ritual abuse survivors of their own abuse. The problem arises when a survivor does not know she has been molested as a child, and she identifies with the images she has of herself as a "pervert." In these cases, the survivor may act on the thoughts of sexual abuse and hurt the child.

The many forms of programming used by cults go against what society labels as normal, acceptable thoughts and behavior. This programming is meant to isolate survivors.

Cults train survivors to keep these programmed thoughts and feelings secret. During the programming, the survivors are told that these "negative" ways of thinking are so bad and evil that if other people knew about these "crazy thoughts," they would hate them and throw them into mental hospitals. Initially, these fear tactics isolate the effects of the programming to specific personalities that do not participate in the survivors' daily lives. By isolating these thoughts and feelings, cults are able to train survivors to look like garden-variety people who have not been traumatized by a violent cult.

When survivors remember the ritual abuse, these tortured and traumatized personalities are finally given a chance to speak. The programming then surfaces in their daily lives because the tortured and traumatized personalities are no longer isolated to their ritual abuse experience. Survivors become plagued with all the thoughts and feelings that were placed in their minds. When survivors understand the effects of programming on their behavior, they are able to break the programming and make their own choices about their lives today.

The point of all programming through torture and hypnosis is centered on forcing the child to rely on the cult. A primary purpose of violent cults is to recruit new members and to keep the ones they already have. It is absolutely essential for survivors and their advocates to remember the intensive and structured brainwashing that is used in the cults to force these children to commit acts of violence. The children may feel ashamed because they hurt about what happened, but they were never shameful for what they were forced to do. Even adults who were brainwashed in cults from the time they were babies, and who are stuck in cults today due to amnesia, have a right to acknowledge their own victimization and seek help. Survivors of ritual abuse who are unconscious of their behavior, and as a result are unable to make choices without being influenced by this intensive cult brainwashing, are also victims and deserve a chance to have their pain heard.

Chapter 5

The Abusers

Most people don't understand the all-encompassing cycle of ritual abuse. They think that getting away from the cults is as simple as making the choice to leave. I know better. Everyone raised in it and entrenched in the way I was knows better.

If you were raised in a cult, leaving is the most painful and difficult thing you will ever do. Not only does the cult come after you most of the time, but you have to worry about your own personalities beings manipulated and tricked into returning. And the isolation and pain you feel as you leave is unbearable. In order to protect themselves, survivors who were raised in cults have to give up their entire family and all their friends to go into a world that, overall, doesn't believe them or support their life changes in a healing manner.

The cult I was raised in has a history. People who are in it today are the modern players of a religion that has been passed on for centuries. My abusers were people. They were not monsters, even though what they did to me was monstrous. Sometimes I saw their aching and longing for change. My cult-boss once told me, "I know what we are doing is wrong, but we don't know how to stop it." Cult abusers are not there because ritual abuse is fun. Many of them are there because they can see no way out.

Many violent cults keep their members by telling them lies that make members feel self-hating and helpless. The lies are difficult to differentiate from truth because the person telling the lies has been brainwashed. Everyone in the cult believes the lies to be truth, and the insanity is passed on from generation to generation as unquestionable wisdom.

I support survivors who hate their abusers. I respect survivors who swear to themselves they will never turn out like the people who hurt them. I do not want to deny survivors their right to feel angry. This anger is justified; it is what gives us the power to change. But I also want people to understand that for too many survivors, ritual abuse victimization does not end in childhood.

CHILDREN WHO ARE TRAINED TO BE ABUSIVE

Cults that ritually abuse children set up situations in which children are forced to molest and sometimes kill other children. Ritually abused children are drugged, lied to, emotionally tormented, and manipulated with threats until they commit the violent acts. Children who react to their orders with fear or sorrow are taunted and humiliated by other group members. The children have no physical escape from the room in which the violence occurs. They have no choice but to comply with the demands of their abusers.

Ritually abused children in these situations must adapt. They stop feeling their initial emotions of fear and grief and replace these appropriate emotions with behavior modeled by their abusers. They learn to laugh at victims who writhe in pain. They make fun of people who are crying or afraid. They adopt the belief systems of their abusers in order to avoid more pain. These children are not bad. They are not evil. They are in a situation that they cannot change, and they do whatever they have to in order to survive.

If the children continue to be exposed to the cult environment, they grow up to act abusively in cults. Because they were raised in cults where they were forced to abuse others, these trained abusers' minds are no longer their own. Even though they abuse children in rituals—with no visible coercion—they are still controlled by the cult. All the years of torture, training, and manipulation are the unseen coercion that makes adult cult members feel helpless to change.

Here is one personality's memory of the process:

> I never abused animals or children outside of the cult experience. Most of my rage and hatred was vented on the men I dated. I would fantasize about killing them, but I never acted violently. I was afraid of being thrown in jail. I was afraid of people hating me. My cult deliberately programmed me never to be violent outside of the cult experience. This

kept me from giving away any secrets about the cult. It made me able to hold respectable roles in the community.

I never remembered the ritual abuse in my daily life. If the cult wanted to talk to me, they had to access me using triggers to speak to my cult personalities. I was primarily involved in cult activities that took place in the middle of the night.

Getting ready for a ritual was like going to the bathroom in the middle of the night. I woke up in a seemingly hypnotic state. I wasn't excited. I didn't feel anything. I was a zombie acting on orders. Once I arrived at a ritual, I felt at home. I felt a final sense of relief and belonging, that I no longer had to hide anything or pretend I was something I was not. It felt great to finally be in my cult personalities, and I didn't have to worry about censoring their thoughts and feelings. Talking to my cult friends before ritual was often a very enjoyable experience.

The rituals themselves varied a great deal. Usually, we just waited for orders about what ritual we were going to perform that evening. Those in charge told us to change into costumes and to put on our makeup. Sometimes we performed skits. Other times we did elaborate ceremonies to celebrate holidays. Sometimes we singled out a member for torture and programming. Everything seemed planned and organized, as if there were some script somewhere that we had to follow.

The ritual itself was extremely emotional. People cried, screamed, or laughed. Sometimes rituals were based on fertility and love. In these rituals, there was no violence. We watched two people who seemed to be truly in love court one another. At other times, we watched the same two people torture and betray each other. Rituals always seemed to end in pain and betrayal. It was people's nightmares coming true.

After the ritual was cleanup. They taught us to be immaculate. As a child, I had to scrub the blood off the floor in the bathroom for hours even after there was not a trace of anything left. They had me scrape under my fingernails. Cleanup was the most painful part of the ritual for me.

After I was cleaned up, I went home and crawled back
into bed. Usually, I was only gone for two or three hours,
from around 1 A.M. to 4 A.M. I always wondered why I needed
ten to twelve hours of sleep a night. Now that I am out of the
cult, I get by on just eight hours of sleep.

ADULTS WHO RITUALLY ABUSE CHILDREN

Behavioral geneticists say that our genetic makeup mutually inter-
acts with our experiences to determine our behavior. Some ritual
abusers are biologically predisposed toward aggressive behavior;
other ritual abusers are genetically timid. But biology is only a frac-
tion of what contributes to human behavior. In the case of ritual
abuse, the environment creates abusers. No matter what a person's
biological predisposition, the cult forces both adults and children
to hurt others. Even adult ritual abusers are victimized by other
adults. Adults who do not act abusively during rituals are taunted
and humiliated just like children.

Adult ritual abusers fall into four primary categories. Some
adult abusers are amnesic of their cult involvement. Other adults
were indoctrinated into the group by the use of unsavory tactics.
The following section describes adult ritual abusers in detail.

Adults Raised in Cults and Currently Amnesic

It appears that most adults who are in these cults today were raised
in them and don't remember having been abused. They dissociated
from the ritual abuse when it was happening, developing multiple
personalities. As adults, they have personalities who still return to
the cult. In their daily lives, however, they are amnesic of their current cult involvement.

These survivors are unable to leave the cults because of amnesia. Clearly, if you're not aware of the abuse until it is happening,
you can't protect yourself from tactics used by the cult to control
your behavior.

Most of these adult cult members spent the first eighteen years
of their lives being brainwashed by the cults. The cults deliberately
attempted to create unconditionally loyal personalities in these

survivors in order to control them for the rest of their lives. The group is able to access amnesic survivors by triggering them with information they received under torture. After the survivors are triggered, they have no memory of their behavior. The cults also programmed these survivors to think in self-destructive ways, to believe they are innately defective—misfits in the world. They are programmed to believe the only people who care about them are current cult members. The amnesia they experience in their daily lives, along with this programmed emotional bondage, keeps these members from planning an escape.

The amnesic members of cults are extremely traumatized, physically and emotionally. They did whatever they had to do in order to survive. These people had no choice but to conform to the beliefs of the group. Some personalities in their multiple systems have internalized the belief systems of the group. The cult is the home of these personalities, who will do anything to protect their home. They are desperate to justify their cult life, which they feel utterly helpless to change.

Adults Raised in Cults and Not Currently Amnesic

Some adults who were raised in these cults do remember their childhood ritual abuse and are also aware of their current cult involvement. These cult members are permanently in the cult personalities formed during their own trauma. These survivors are stuck in cults for the same reasons as amnesic survivors, except these people are aware of their dilemma. They are in the cult as a result of their own childhood trauma. They didn't choose to join a group that ritually abuses children. This way of life was forced on them. Although they remember their current cult involvement, they are still multiples who are controlled by intensive programming.

Amnesic Adults Who Were Ritually Abused as Children and Joined a Violent Group as an Adult

The third type of abuser consists of adults who were raised in cults, but don't remember it. Later in life, they may inadvertently join a group that ritually abuses children. Some adult survivors actively seek out groups that practice violent rituals. Others join secret societies or fraternal organizations for business opportunities and are pulled into a violent cult through the intensive indoctrination procedure.

At the beginning of the indoctrination process, new members are taught to tolerate differences in religious beliefs. The new members read about a variety of religious belief systems, which leads them to question their own moral and religious beliefs. At this vulnerable point, cults require members to read about cultures that practiced adult and child sacrifices. Slowly, the members learn a belief system that allows them to justify the use of violence during rituals.

As these adult ritual abuse survivors learn about the violent belief system of the group, they resonate with beliefs reminiscent of their own childhood ritual abuse. For the first time in their lives, the deepest trauma in their experience, their own abuse—even though they don't consciously remember it—is finally being talked about and justified on a philosophical level.

Next, these new members witness or participate in moderately sexualized, violent rituals. First, they may see an animal sacrificed in a ritual performed by the group. The group justifies the act based on the previously learned philosophies. For example, the group may tell the new member that the animal was not killed, but rather it was sacrificed in order to teach all the members of the group about the natural process of life and death. Naked women may also be present at the ritual as a symbol of the purity of our natural birth form. After the new member participates in a sexualized, violent ritual and crosses the first line breaking standard morality, the group then has the most effective tactic to keep the person loyal and silent. The group may threaten to tell the new member's family about his or her participation in the violent rituals.

Most violent occult groups require members to work through degrees or levels. As they graduate to higher levels, members learn more about the philosophy and the structure of the group as a whole, and rituals become more violent. Eventually, they learn to question every aspect of standard morality, and to accept more justifications for violence and group sexual acts. The more violence the members see in rituals, the more intense are the threats to remain silent.

Because these people are aware of their current cult involvement, but unaware of their own ritual abuse history, they are easily manipulated by the cults. They not only feel the guilt and shame for their present behavior, but they also feel an intense unidentified deeper shame that is a result of their own ritual abuse. This shame is what keeps them trapped.

Adults Who Were Not Ritually Abused and Who Join Violent Cults

The final group is adult cult members who were not ritually abused as children. Some of these people are pulled into violent cults through the intensive indoctrination process described above. Because the systematic violence that occurs in cults would be difficult for anyone who was not extremely dissociative to witness, it is likely that these people must have been exposed to a major trauma at some point in their lives—such as incest or parental abuse—that made them numb and vulnerable to the lure of extreme sexualized violence.

EMOTIONAL EXPERIENCES OF ABUSERS

Ritual abusers themselves have undergone emotional experiences that allow them to act violently and abusively. Commonly, abusers suffer from loss of love, lack of emotion, and numbness.

Loss of Love

Love allows us to feel compassion and warmth for others. It is the emotion that must be silenced in order to create abusers. Most cult programming is designed to destroy the spontaneity of feeling love for oneself and others.

What is so powerful about the experience of love that the cult must destroy it to create abusers? Love is the fullness we feel in our hearts and the warmth that draws us to other people. It is the yearning we feel deep inside that makes us want to be right next to the people who make us feel good inside. Love is about understanding and giving. No love is more powerful than the love we first felt for ourselves. The fullness belonged to us, and anything that threatened to take it away became "bad." Anything that threatened to hurt our hearts, making us feel the less comfortable emotions of anger, fear, and sorrow, became our own inner sense of what was "evil."

This fullness was a daily part of our lives as children. Along with the fullness came the intensity of all the other feelings when the fullness was threatened. We felt anger, the love of ourselves that said, "Don't take this feeling of love away!" We felt fear, which said, "My existence is threatened," and told the body to move and find protection. We felt the sorrow that lets us know something has been lost, that tells us the fullness cannot always be, but we can cry about it and give ourselves room to feel it once again. If we don't feel the anger that says, "Stop!", if we don't feel the fear that says, "Get me out of here!", if we don't feel the sorrow that says, "It won't change. This hurts!", then there is never room for the fullness to return.

Children abused in these violent cults are constantly told to not feel. They are taught that love is about betrayal. They are laughed at when they show their affection for others. Most Christian-based cults teach that the only true love is the amorphous, undefined love of God or Jesus. By discounting or not allowing the children to feel the love inside their hearts—and by labeling love as a spiritual concept out of their reach—the children become isolated from the self-protective power of their own emotions. They are never allowed to feel the fullness that gives all the other emotions room to emerge.

Children abused in these cults are not allowed to feel sad. When they cry, others make fun of them. Sorrow is a sign of weakness in the eyes of the abusers. If you show other people that something has hurt you, you are made to feel worse. Ritually abused children are not allowed to feel happy either. The cults tell the children that they have no right to smile when so many people in the world are suffering. For example, during a violent ritual scene, they tell a child who has found a few moments of relief playing in the corner, "How can you smile and laugh when your friend is being tortured?"

Children abused in these cults are not allowed to feel fear. The abuse itself initially causes intense fear in the victims. The only way children survive the attacks is to stop the fear from overwhelming them. Children who are abused in these violent cults never feel safe from the abusers. If the children allowed themselves to feel their fear, they would be afraid constantly.

Finally, even though the activities of these cults are fueled by anger, children in the cults are taught when to be angry and who to be angry with. Anger is not allowed to be an expression of self-protection. The cults only allow anger if it is expressed in ways that are socially acceptable to the group. In the cults, anger is the emotion the cults manipulate to force the children to commit acts of violence. For example, after a child expresses anger at the abusers, the cult forces her to vent the rage onto an innocent victim.

Because the children are never allowed to feel their true emotions, soon they learn not to feel at all. What they feel inside their hearts becomes silent and numb. Their minds tell them what they feel without any input from their emotions. This leaves the children open to any mental manipulation used by the cult to control their behavior.

Lack of Emotion

Ritual abuse causes physiological changes in the body that result in a lack of emotional sensation. When children experience no emotions, they are easily manipulated by the controlling adults.

Here's a personal reflection from a survivor:

> I can tell you that I experience feelings from my brain, but I rarely experience feelings inside my body. From my Adam's apple to my navel, I am empty. When I say I am angry, it is a thought in my brain. There is rarely a tightening in my chest or a physical sensation that I identify that goes along with the thought. Only a few times a month do I feel sensations in my chest area, and almost always they are painful feelings of aching or tightening that are short in duration.
>
> My inability to feel is the most devastating result of the trauma. I am hollow and empty. As a child, I do remember feelings in my chest area. I can remember aching and hurting

so bad, swearing that I would never be hurt like that again. Well, my prayers were answered.

I know what it would take to bring feeling back into that area. I can feel sensations start sometimes when I talk about the ritual abuse. It always starts with the most uncomfortable tension and pain, not felt in my chest area, but rather it feels like a huge presence outside of me that is trying to push its way into me. And as it moves in, I get headaches and a dull, poisonous pain in all the cells of my body. The discomfort is unbearable, nothing seems to soothe it, and I still don't feel a solid emotion in my chest that would allow me to relieve the pain by screaming, raging, or crying.

If I can wait out the escalating pain and discomfort for days, something that is impossible for me to do when I have to put on a chipper face to go to work, finally emotion emerges in my chest area. Then I feel alive. The process is worth that feeling of life, but the process is also impossible when there is no safety in my life allowing me to experience the first initial sensations of anxiety and discomfort.

Without our feelings, we have no reason to wake up in the morning, no reason to deal with any of the injustices that happen to us in the world. Our feelings are what give us the motivation to find happiness and justice. For many people, the emptiness inside makes them feel like they might as well be dead. If nothing felt good, ever, would it be worth it to stay alive and struggle just to survive? Many survivors of ritual abuse face this question every day.

Numbness

Survivors are triggered by experiences that remind them of the ritual abuse. When this happens, the lack of emotion turns into an uncomfortable numb sensation. Numbness is literally a numb, dead, tingly, sensation that covers unbearable pain. The numb sensation is more uncomfortable than no emotions, driving survivors to try to experience some kind of genuine emotion or physical sensation. It's not surprising that survivors often turn to addictions when the numb sensation emerges. Drugs, overeating, sexual acting-out, and so on temporarily relieve the numbness and return the body to the state of no emotions.

At times, such as when a memory of abuse surfaces, the numb sensation becomes so strong that nothing can stop it. Sometimes victims feel a desire to reenact their own abuse to alleviate the numbness. Hurting others makes them feel closer to the parts of themselves that disassociated during their own trauma. Abusers finally see their own pain reflected on the face of their victims. Instead of actually remembering their own pain and victimization, they connect to their own pain by witnessing it in someone else. Although the feelings abusers experience after committing a sexually violent act are not necessarily pleasurable, for some abusers stopping the numb feeling outweighs the later pangs of guilt. However, by not honestly confronting their victimization and pain, abusers never find relief. They compulsively continue to victimize others, with no end to their suffering.

THE ABUSERS OF SURVIVORS

More than half of the survivors in this study said their abusers were their parents (see Table 5.1). Our relationships with our family members are our primary relationships. The fact that parents can ritually abuse their own children, betraying their most intimate relationships, indicates just how isolated and disconnected abusers are from their feelings.

Nearly all of the identified abusers were functioning members of their communities (see Table 5.2). In light of the dynamics of

Table 5.1   The Perpetrators of the Ritual Abuse

Fathers	67%	Uncles	27%
Mothers	42%	Physicians (not family)	33%
Grandfathers	31%	Priests/Ministers (not family)	17%
Grandmothers	23%	Teacher (not family)	17%
Aunts	21%		

Table 5.2   Occupations of Fathers Identified as Perpetrators of Ritual Abuse

Attorney	Mechanical engineers (2)
Building contractor	Medical professional
Chemist	Miner
Electrical, chemical, and mechanical engineer	Phone company employee
	Physician
Electrical engineer	Plumber
Factory workers (2)	Realtor
Farmer	Salesman
Fence builder	Semiskilled laborer
File clerk	Steel mill manager
Foreman electrician	Supervisor of projection department
Government worker	Taxi driver
High-security government employee in computer technology	Teacher
	Upholsterer
Hydro worker	U.S. Army officer
Locksmith	Vice-president of a New York City bank
Manager of a grange store	

Occupations of Mothers Identified as Perpetrators of Ritual Abuse

Beauticians (3)	Sales clerk
Housewives (6)	Secretary
Locksmith	Teachers (2)
Mechanical engineer	Teacher for emotionally disturbed children
Occupational therapist for emotionally disturbed children	Waitress

Occupations of Other Identified Perpetrators

Auto mechanic	Bishop
Bartender	Carpenter

Chauffeur

Computer programmer

Construction worker

Day-care coordinator

Educational recruiter

Electrician

Engineer

Executive secretary

Factory workers

Farmers

Foreman

High school principal

Institutionalized in a psychiatric hospital

Insurance salesman

Judges

Lawyers

Medical professionals

Mental health professional

Morticians

Nurse

Owned a produce company

Pharmaceutical clerk

Psychiatrists

Police officers

Politicians

Postmaster

Professor

Ranchers

School library superintendent

Security guard

State trooper

Students

Sunday school teacher

Traveling recruiter

Unemployed

U.S. Air Force, top security clearance

U.S. Army generals

Veterinarians

Weatherman

Similar Occupations of Perpetrators of Ritual Abuse

Physicians	35%	Priests/Ministers	22%
Teachers	25%	Police officers	15%

disassociation, it is not surprising that ritual abuse perpetrators are able to function so well. It is their ability not to feel that makes them capable of going to work during the day and torturing or killing people at night. If they did feel their emotions, they would be unable to function in the world but would also be unable to participate in the ritual abuse of children.

AT WHAT AGE WERE SURVIVORS ABUSED?

Many violent cults start torturing and brainwashing victims when they are still unable to talk. For most survivors, the abuse continues until they are removed from the abusive environment. Some survivors never were removed from the abusive environment and continued to be abused until they were in their twenties, thirties, and forties. Two survivors said the abuse was still happening today (see Tables 5.3 and 5.4).

Although a small percentage of the survivors in this study did say the abuse was still happening, other survivors reported being severely revictimized when they were falsely accused of ongoing cult involvement.

> I asked a minister to officiate at a funeral/memorial service for my babies that had been sacrificed in rituals. I did this last year in hopes of putting some closure on the painful issue of my babies, and also it would give me a ceremony/ritual to honor them and say goodbye. The minister anonymously turned me into the police for child abuse, and an investigative team came out to my house because they had been told I was sacrificing babies in my home. They assessed the report was untrue. Because I speak in the community about ritual abuse, the police felt this report to be a threat and that I might be in danger. They taught me how to protect myself, but for three days my daughter and I lived in terror. Finally, my therapist and I put the pieces together and guessed it could only be this minister. I confronted the minister, who admitted being the one making the report. There was a semi-apology made, but the minister felt she had to protect herself, both from me and any cult I might be involved in. She had *no* understanding of what it is to be a child victim. This ordeal was so traumatic for me that I've not yet been able to approach anyone else to perform the ceremony I still feel I want and need.

THE QUESTION OF RESPONSIBILITY

Young children cannot be expected to protect themselves. They do not have the power to change the world in order for them to be safe.

Table 5.3   Age at Which the Abuse Began (in years)

0 to 3	65%	10 to 11	4%
4 to 5	12%	12 to 13	0%
6 to 7	8%	14 to 15	2%
8 to 9	0%	Do not know	9%

Table 5.4   Age at Which the Abuse Ended (in years)

5 to 10	21%	31 to 35	2%
11 to 15	29%	36 to 40	4%
16 to 20	14%	Reports of abuse today	4%
21 to 25	8%	Do not know	14%
26 to 30	4%		

Only adults have this power. Adults are the ones who are responsible for protecting children.

All people who commit injustices against other people, consciously or unconsciously, have a responsibility to the victims and to themselves. The act of violation leads to isolation and pain. People who have made mistakes and have violated others need to find the strength to heal their own wounds and take care of themselves. Only when they have taken care of themselves are they genuinely able to give to others. A drowning person cannot throw a child a life preserver.

After taking care of themselves, after creating a safe, gentle place of compassion inside themselves for themselves, abusers can begin to look outward to those they have hurt. They can genuinely right the wrongs they have committed. The most wonderful gift an abuser can give to a victim is the truth, a complete confession owning all responsibility for the abuse.

Next comes financial responsibility for the damage inflicted on the victim. Some abusers unconditionally provide funding for the victim's therapy. An abuser who cannot support the victim financially can find other ways to help in the healing process.

Never did the victim cause the abuse. The abuser is *always* the one responsible. Abusers must find the courage to heal themselves. It is through their healing that abusers are able to mend the separation they feel from other people.

SUMMARY OF KEY POINTS

Children from all around the United States are telling us that they have been systematically abused during rituals. Adults suffering from the same traumatic symptoms as war veterans and torture survivors say they were abused in violent rituals. Both adult and child survivors of ritual abuse who remember the violence experience flashbacks and become overwhelmed with physical and emotional pain.

In nearly all cases, the victims report they were abused by two or more adults. Some people report they grew up in a cult and unwillingly continued to be a cult member as an adult. These survivors were traumatized by systematic brainwashing and torture into an unwanted amnesia of their behavior. They formed multiple personalities, some of which are controlled by the cult, and these programmed personalities return to the cult to avoid further torture and emotional cruelty.

Most people involved in violent cults would not choose to be there. If they could find a way out, they would leave. Many of the current members of violent cults were raised in cults and are unable to get out due to amnesia, threats, and trauma. The remaining members were indoctrinated into the belief system when they joined a secret society or fraternal organization. Threats of harm to themselves or to their families prevent them from leaving the group.

Violent cults are extremely sadistic, and abusers appear to take pleasure in other people's pain. Sadistic pleasure is a result of disassociation, which stops numbness and their own memories of abuse. Cult involvement is a victimizing experience for all members. Most people are forced to be there. After members relinquish hope for change in their own lives, they try to pull others into the same misery. On an unspoken level, they believe that if they have to be in the cult and be as miserable as they are, at least they are not in it alone.

Chapter 6

The Groups: Beliefs, Practices, History, and Structure

My abusers taught me that people of this world are ruled by the God of Abraham, the God of the Old Testament. His laws are unjust laws based on the rules of nature. He teaches an eye for an eye, a tooth for a tooth. He is the God of Ignorance, the God of Violence and lower Intelligence. In his world, people suffer. In his world, there is chaos, plague, and starvation. His world is in the desert.

In our belief system, the ultimate deity is the God manifested in the actions of Jesus. We believe Jesus was not a doctor or a magician who healed physical blindness. He healed the blindness of the spirit, a feat far greater than the acts of any doctor or magician. He said the words that our hearts longed to hear. He spoke the Truth. But when he died, so did his Word. Once again, the Word was lost.

We believe Jesus's teachings should not be dictated by some "church." Morality is not something we learn intellectually. It is something we each must emotionally experience. We believe people must find the truth inside themselves if they want to understand from their hearts what Jesus was trying to say. We designed rituals and systems of thought to help people realize the deep revelations Jesus spoke about. We believe that in order to learn the Truth found in his words, people must lose the Truth in their own lives. In other words, in order to have compassion for people who are hungry, you must have experienced hunger yourself. In order to have compassion for people who are freezing on the street, you also must have felt bitterly cold.

We believe that through Jesus radiated the perfect emanation of Heavenly Light. The heavenly light is also symbolized in the Old Testament of the Judeo-Christian Bible as Lucifer, the Light Bearer, the serpent who enticed Eve to eat from the Tree of Knowledge. Religions based on the teachings of the Old Testament referred to Lucifer as Satan or the Devil because he led people astray from the teachings of the God of Abraham. In our teachings, Lucifer was not the "Devil." He was the Bringer of Light, the bringer of wisdom, which allowed humankind the opportunity to overcome the laws of nature. He was the bringer of knowledge, which allowed humankind the ability to judge the world from something other than our immediate experiences. He told us to eat from the Tree of Knowledge of Good and Evil so we could know what was right and wrong and could see the Laws of the Ignorant God are Unjust.

We most certainly would not consider ourselves to be Satan worshipers. We believe that "Satan" is a term used by the church to separate the world into good and evil through the eyes of the God of the Old Testament. In our belief system, Satan—or the personification of evil—is Ignorance. It is only a shadow, a temporary stage of thought before Revelation. Only love, light, and truth exist. Everything else is a mistake, a shadow, an "accident." That is why we believe that we can commit any act without feeling shame or remorse. Our philosophy says, "Nothing can be created that is not God."

We symbolize the loss of the Word in a number of ways: the death of Osiris in the Egyptian myth, which leaves Isis weeping and yearning for her lost husband; the quest for the Holy Grail, which contains the water that gives eternal life. The acts we commit during rituals intensify the power of this imagery. No one yearns for the water or the Word more than someone who each day is having it taken away.

We believe we have to create the perfect race: a race of warriors to prepare for his second coming. We don't know where he is going to be born. We don't know where the Word is going to become manifest, but we have to make a people that is going to be ready to hear the message.

This is what they taught me. They used this philosophy to manipulate and control me time and time again. For people who believe only love, light, and truth exist, they certainly did everything in their power to see that I never felt loved.

My abusers taught me that our mission is to unite all humankind under a single principle. They used a great deal of symbolism to describe that principle, but they would never say what it was. Due to my own past and what I knew was important to me, I always assumed that principle was love. I actually found support for my theory in some cult philosophy.

When I told my idea to them, they led me to believe I had found the supreme secret. They told me they do what they do to make people value the importance of love. They told me that no one knows more about just how important love is than someone who has had it stolen from their life everyday. In a way, I could see their twisted logic. I knew because I lacked love most of my life, I longed for it desperately.

I saw that my abusers were people in a great deal of pain, but the actions and goals of the group as a whole are not what these men say they are. Ritual abuse is designed to betray love. It makes children so hopeless and despairing that it seems impossible to trust or love again. Ritually abused children learn that love is about suffering and betrayal. Because of the intense programming, they feel alone in a way that almost can't be comforted. The only thing that heals these children is love, but—guaranteed—they do not get unbetrayed, supportive love from their abusers. These children heal if they are lucky enough to find someone or something special enough to them that they are able to break the walls of their isolation.

Ritual abuse hurts children almost beyond repair. The messages the cults give children about love cause them to be so terrified of failure, betrayal, humiliation, and unrequited love, that often they just push love out of their life.

No, the goal is not to unite people under the concept of love. The goal, as dictated by their actions, is to teach people that love is a weakness; that love only ends in pain and loss. They show their victims that life is tragic, and they make the children believe there is no love to protect "bad" children abused in cults. They conclude the world is not a place guided by a benevolent force that wants all people to feel love and pleasure. Rather, the universe is guided by rules and logic, and love is the folly that corrupts people to commit foolish acts that result in pain.

What is life without love? How do we feel when we believe no one loves us? How do we feel when we believe the universe is based *only on rules and logic and no other forces? If love is a folly that leads to despair and suffering, then how do we treat those around us? How deeply do we hurt when we are alone? If the universe was based only on rules and logic, we would not have emotions.*

Whether there is a God or not, whether the universe is benevolent or malevolent, human beings have the right to choose what feels best. If we live in a world where love has no place, would we still want to be here? If we lived in a world where love had no limits, where betrayal was unheard of because everyone wanted to feel good, what would life be like? If there was no such thing as unrequited love, and we could love to our heart's content without ever having to worry about being hurt, what a place this would be! So I believe it is a choice of what we value in our own lives, God or no God, benevolent or malevolent universe. No matter what abusers or anyone may take away, we can still look inside and listen to what makes us feel good.

BELIEF SYSTEMS OF VIOLENT CULTS

Violent cults that ritually abuse children use a variety of belief systems to justify their acts. Some belief systems are based on the idea of needing to understand both good and evil in order to reach spiritual enlightenment. In violent cults based on this belief, members engage in all evil acts imaginable in an attempt to understand the nature of evil.

Some violent cults believe in supreme evil powers or beings that can be worshiped to gain supernatural power. Under this belief system, people practice ritual abuse as a means to worship the evil forces or personifications.

Other belief systems are based on the idea of creating a superior white race to rule the world. These cults believe they must torture and ritually abuse their children in order to create a "stronger" breed of humans that can withstand any degree of pain.

Still other belief systems teach children Christian morals using violent tactics.

Finally, some belief systems are based on worshiping the cycles of nature. These violent cults teach that death, pain, and destruction are all natural cycles of existence that must be worshiped the same as life, joy, and creation. Cults that ritually abuse children usually have belief systems based on one or more of these theoretical foundations.

Ritual abuse occurs under a variety of different religious beliefs—from satanism to Christianity, from paganism to white supremacy. It is important to remember that not all followers of these belief systems are involved in ritual abuse. There are people who call themselves satanists who don't practice ritual abuse, just as there are Christians who don't practice ritual abuse. There are also people who call themselves witches who worship the Great Goddess, and people who believe strongly in the power of magic, who have never used violence as part of their rituals. The following section describes only the groups within these traditions that practice ritual abuse. The source of this information is from my own personal experience, as well as from conversations I have had with other ritual abuse survivors.

The Unifying God

The idea of reuniting the dualistic concepts of good and evil is a common philosophy used by groups that practice ritual abuse. The groups suggest that behind good and evil is a single Source from which both good and evil sprang. They suggest that if humankind finds that Source, we will obtain world peace, universal religion, and harmony.

In practice, how does a group search for the source of good in the world? How does a group search for the source of evil? Some groups believe that in order to find the Source, they must engage in all acts considered both good and evil. They believe that if they examine good and evil intellectually, without practicing the acts, they could not evoke emotion and truly reveal the Source.

In order to understand such a belief system, it is important to understand the philosophical image of "the unifying God." In such a belief system, there is no duality, and hence no true evil. The unifying God encompasses both good and evil. Some groups symbolize the unifying God as unconditional love because unconditional love feels warmth for everything, without judgment. In a unifying God belief system, God's presence is in everything. God is not separate from our lives. Taking this belief a step further, if everything is God, nothing can be created that is not God. Therefore, evil does not really exist because it is part of God.

Worship of Evil

Devil worship, black magic, and other practices used to worship evil are all attempts to gain power by connecting with a dark force. In these belief systems, there is an evil force, energy, or personification in the universe that can be used for personal gain. Worshipers believe that the darker force of the universe provides people with immense power. Usually, these people desire things that are associated with the concept of evil: power over others, sexual gratification without love. Over half of the survivors who participated in this study said they had been abused by a satanic cult.

People who worship evil have their behavior dictated to them by the image they have of the evil force. For example, a devil worshiper who feels compassion or love for someone who is being harmed during a ritual is unable to stop what is happening or cry in remorse because such "moral" behavior is not acceptable to the group. It is reminiscent of the Good God's tenets of morality.

White Supremacy

Many violent cults also teach a doctrine of white supremacy. They ritually abuse their children in an attempt to create a superior white race that will overtake the world. These groups are bonded by a mutual hatred for an identified race or group of people. This immature type of bonding, based on victimizing other people, provides white supremacists with a sense of belonging. If they can identify a common enemy, then they are able to feel bonded to the group and they no longer feel alone in the world. If they all hate blacks, Jews, or homosexuals, they feel as though they have something in common with one another. They will violate anyone's rights whenever needed in order to feel this immature sense of belonging.

Belief in Magic

The belief in magic is a central feature of ritual abuse. According to *The New Merriam-Webster Dictionary,* magic is the art of people who claim to be able to do things by the help of supernatural powers or by their own knowledge of nature's secrets.[1] My abusers taught me that magic is the ability to shape reality according to your will. Some ancient magical teachings suggest that through pain and suffering, people are able to connect to higher planes of spiritual reality. In a sense, the magicians of the past were correct. Psychologists who study perception say that our perception is a result of biochemical operations within the brain. Trauma alters brain chemistry, which results in changed perceptions of reality.

When a child is tortured, his or her body releases adrenaline and endorphins as a response to the stress. These substances alter the biochemistry in the child's mind and may cause hallucinations. For example, a pin that is dropped on the other side of the room may sound to a child in this state like a thunderbolt. From an ancient magician's point of view, the child's experience is a mystical one.

Hundreds of years ago, under this type of magical belief system, people tortured themselves and others for a perceived spiritual benefit. They did not understand dissociation, amnesia, and multiple personalities as defense mechanisms that allowed people to survive the pain; they believed these responses to severe trauma to be "magic." The perceived power of early magicians who traumatized children was unimaginable. They were thought to have mystical power over people. But in all truth, they were the causes of children's dissociation, the brain's response to trauma.

Christianity

Christian-based ritual abuse is one of most confusing forms of abuse. The abusers teach children strict moral principles of honesty, integrity, and nonviolent behavior, while they are being ritually abused. Children are taught that violence is acceptable in the ritual context because it is being used for higher spiritual purposes. The most confusing part is that the abusers actually believe the ritual abuse is helpful for children. They believe that the values of honesty, integrity, and nonviolent behavior must be taught to children through violence. In the case of molestation, they might say the children need to share their bodies with others as a pure, Christian gesture. If they are unable to rationalize the abuse, they blame their violent impulses on the devil.

As a result of the ritual abuse, children raised in these cults may develop aggressive, sexualized, sadistic tendencies that the abusers frame as "evil" and "sinful" impulses. These children grow up feeling that they have a hidden evil inside of them. They often try desperately to follow Christian values, but instead are attracted to sexual violence. Many of these adults constrain their violent impulses until they get to a ritual, where they explode with sexually violent behavior. If they act sexually or violently outside of a ritual context, they are often plagued with extreme guilt and blame their acts on Satan.

Female Cults

One of the most secretive contexts for ritual abuse is in female cults. These groups do not allow men and usually are based on the worship of the cycles of nature. They believe that death and destruction are natural parts of the cycle of existence and must be worshiped the same as life and creation. Just as there are many Christians who do not practice violence in their rituals, there are also a number of women around the country who refer to themselves as witches and worship the cycles of nature who do not engage in ritual abuse. This is an important distinction to make because traditionally, as exemplified by the Inquisition, "witches" are often the people accused of practicing violence during their rituals.

The female cults that do practice ritual abuse are extremely secretive. Female cults preach that men are the cause of the problems on the earth. They are responsible for the destruction of the planet. They remind members that for the most part, ever since humans devised the concept of ownership, men have claimed they own their Mother Earth (in the form of property), their wives, and their children. In order to satisfy their ownership desires, men kicked the feminine out of people's understanding of "God." Men taught people to refer to God as a male figure in the sky so they could violate the earth. Women were kept in the home, silent. Female cults also remind their members that within the last century, since women have increased their power in our society, major reforms have occurred to protect the earth, women, and children. Often women feel bonded to their female cults because they see the accuracy in such statements.

Female cults primarily worship the feminine principle in the form of the Great Goddess. When they worship the male force, they usually worship him as a passive force that is in service to her. Sometimes he is gentle and compassionate, not violent and in search of power. Other times he is the Reaper, the power of destruction that takes life away from the earth. They worship the love between the God and the Goddess as a sexualized union that creates life. They believe that the love between the Goddess and her consort, the God, is the force that holds all life together.

The Goddess has three faces, which are all worshiped in violent female cults. Although there is a great deal of variety, I will describe some of the practices I am familiar with. The first face, creation, is worshiped with rites of fertility. These rituals are sexual and moderately violent. An animal might be killed to remind members that for something to live, something else must die. Next is the face of destruction. These rituals are extremely violent and are designed to connect members to their most cruel and sadistic impulses. Children or babies might be killed. Members are forced to suffer because destruction causes pain. Finally, there is the face of rebirth or rest, depending on the cult. These rituals also include violence and sexuality. Rebirth in female cults usually involves mock killings accompanied by sexual unions, to symbolize that death is not the end, but the beginning of a new life. Female cults are the most secretive. No males are allowed to witness the rites except for the young sons of members.

Most female cult members were also raised in male/female cults. Female cult hatred for men is based on the practices of the male/female cults. In male/female cults, men are taught to betray, humiliate, and degrade women. Women are taught to be loving and unconditionally loyal to the men, no matter how great the betrayal may be. In their daily lives, female cult members are usually attracted to male cult members because they can understand each others' pain. In cult members' relationships, programming about how to behave surfaces and female hatred for men intensifies. Female cult beliefs about men as "evil, snakes" is thus supported, because neither partner is able to identify the ritual abuse as the cause of the problems in the relationship.

RITUALS

This section is based on my own memories and on conversations I have had with other survivors. Although some of the practices of violent cults might be similar to practices of nonviolent groups, it is important to remember that the differentiating factor between the cults described in this book and other cults is that the cults described in this book practice violence while children are present.

Rituals are structured events in which members are assigned roles. Usually, someone leads the rituals. Most leaders are referred to as High Priests or High Priestesses. High Priests, High Priestesses, or both simultaneously lead prayers, perform sacrifices, and engage in sexual acts, while other members witness or participate. The exact activities of a particular ritual vary, depending on the holiday.

Some rituals are fertility rites. During these ceremonies, members engage in sexual orgies, using perfumes and oils to enhance stimulation. People wear luxurious clothing and eat extravagant foods as a means to celebrate prosperity and earthly delights. Most cults celebrate spring rituals, such as May Day and the Vernal Equinox, with fertility rites.

Other rituals are based on the principles of life and death. In these ceremonies, animals or humans are sacrificed. Cult members drain the blood of the creatures and use it as body paints or drink. Most human sacrifices performed during rituals are mock sacrifices, in which High Priests or Priestesses dramatize the sacrifice of children or adults. Babies taken from members are the most common real human sacrifices. Actual human sacrifice of children and adults may also be performed, but only on special occasions. Mock killings are performed more often and are designed to look as believable as real killings. Cults use the blood of animals to enhance the effect of agony and suffering. For young children, witnessing mock killings is sometimes just as psychologically damaging as witnessing the genuine killing of humans. A child who watches a friend being killed in a ritual, and then later sees the friend playing with other people, learns that death is not "real." Life and death are blended, and the child no longer understands the significance of either.

Some rituals are designed to train members for special roles. Training rituals are not performed on specific holidays, but whenever members are available. Training rituals generally include performances, in which members wear elaborate costumes, and may also include fertility rites and sacrifices.

Holidays   *Christmas – child – winter*

The holidays celebrated by violent cults vary a great deal depending on the cult's specific belief system. However, most cults in the United States recognize the spring and autumn equinoxes (March and September 21) and the winter and summer solstices (June and December 21). Cult members believe these holidays give them power by connecting them with the forces of nature.

Most cults also celebrate the Christian holidays of Christmas and Easter. Many cults recognize Jesus as a supreme symbol for good, and celebrating his birth and death is believed to enhance the power of the group.

Some cults also celebrate Beltane (April 30), a satanic and matriarchal holiday, and the marriage of the Beast (September 7), a satanic holiday. Celebrating satanic holidays allows nonsatanic cults to utilize what they consider "evil" powers as well. Most cults also celebrate the ancient agricultural holidays of Halloween and May Day.

Robes and Costumes

At the beginning of most rituals, participants wear robes or costumes. The color of the robes depends on the ritual and the group. Most groups wear black or white robes for sacrificial rituals, and blue or violet robes for fertility rites. Once the ritual begins, clothing is often removed either simultaneously or as part of a ritual skit.

In my experience, the leaders of male/female cults usually wear tall hats (similar in shape to the hat of the pope) during rituals. The shape and color of hats are used to identify a person's rank in the group. In general, taller hats with more elaborate decoration signify a more important role. During ritual drama, women wear fancy, costumelike dresses. Men wear costumes as well, often with knives and swords attached to uniforms. The clothing is often made of silk, leather, and lace.

Children are usually not allowed to wear clothing during rituals. Sometimes adults wearing clown costumes or Dracula costumes torment the children. Adults also dress up as vicious animals to frighten the children into silence. Often an adult member dresses up as Jesus, and he too betrays the children. These situations are designed to teach children that nothing is safe.

Use of Color and Symbolism

Red and black are the colors of satanic, violent cults. Nonsatanic cults also use these colors because of their "darker" powers. White is a color used by cults to signify innocence and purity. Blue and violet are colors of fertility, with blue as the healing color and violet as the color of love and power. Most cults believe in the spiritual significance of geometrical shapes, particularly the circle, triangle, pentagram, and other stars.

HISTORY OF VIOLENT CULTS

Because I am a survivor of ritual abuse, I wanted to know how long such abuse had been going on. I read a number of books to find out if any other groups historically had practiced rituals similar to the ones I remembered from my own abuse. I don't claim to be an expert on history or religion, but I do feel it is important to present the information I found that helped me believe my own memories of abuse.

Historically, conquering people attempt to convert conquered people to their own religious beliefs, and they persecute those people who continue to practice their old religion. Throughout history, a number of religious groups have been persecuted for their religious beliefs, sometimes with the use of torture and execution. Forcing people to change their religious beliefs is a difficult task. Before the scientific revolution, people's religious beliefs were the most important beliefs they had. The sun rose in the morning because of God. The rains that kept the crops alive and kept the people from starving were also a gift from God. Humankind's entire existence and the world around them was a magical mystery, which they explained using their religious beliefs. Forcing people to change their religious beliefs forced them to change their basic understanding of the world. If people truly believed their religion was the "Truth"—and most religions believe they have the "Truth"— it would follow that some members of a given religion would do whatever they had to in order to preserve it.

It is possible that in some families, the practice of ritual abuse and programming developed during times when it was dangerous for people to express religious convictions that contradicted the religious beliefs of the ruling class. Followers of a persecuted religion who wanted to pass their beliefs on to their children had to do so in secret. They had to worry if their children told the neighbors about their hidden spiritual practices and beliefs, they would be punished, perhaps tortured and killed. To protect themselves, perhaps these desperate parents physically reprimanded their children for telling others about their religious convictions and practices. Historically, there have been no laws to protect children from violence that did not end in death. Perhaps the beatings and teachings parents gave their children became more intense and violent as danger increased. As a result, in some families' religious beliefs, rituals and violence all became intermingled into what we now refer to as ritual abuse.

Once a family is caught in a cycle of extreme violence, it is very difficult to break the pattern. The previous chapter on abusers illustrates that extreme trauma results in a lack of emotion. Often this lack of emotion then results in the capacity to abuse others with no remorse. Due to lack of understanding about the cycle of trauma, people raised in these families were helpless to change their predicament and became stuck in the cycle of ritual abuse.

Ritual Abuse: Children Raised in Violent Belief Systems

Throughout history, a number of religious movements have been accused of practicing violent, sexualized rituals similar to those described by ritual abuse survivors. Certain sects of the Gnostics, a spiritual movement that rivaled the early Catholic church, were accused by the church of practicing violent, sexualized rituals over fifteen hundred years ago. In the Middle Ages, a small number of secret societies and fraternal organizations were also accused of similar acts.

In a paper published in the journal *Dissociation: Progress in the Dissociative Disorders,* Sally Hill and Jean Goodwin noted similarities between the violent rituals that some Gnostic sects were speculated to have practiced and the rituals described by ritual abuse survivors today. Some Gnostic sects were accused of (1) participating in a secret nocturnal feast; (2) reversing the Christian mass; (3) engaging in orgiastic sex involving incest; (4) using blood, semen, and other excretions during rituals; and (5) sacrificing embryos and infants that were later eaten. All of the above accusations have also been described in modern times by ritual abuse survivors.[2]

The Gnostics were divided into a variety of sects that disagreed about practices and beliefs, although they shared some common elements. The sects as a whole believed that the world lived in ignorance. They agreed that human beings lived in an imperfect state and that through Gnosis, a spiritual revelation, humankind could be redeemed to its true spiritual nature. Most sects also believed that the God of the Old Testament was inferior to the Supreme Unknown God of the Universe. They believed that the world of matter—everything physical we experience around us—was infested with the same imperfection as the God of the Old Testament. Since all matter was imperfect, the body itself was also considered imperfect. The only redeeming factor human beings received from the Supreme Unknown God was a single spark of life. A few sects claimed the God of the Old Testament was Satan himself because he punished people with extreme violence, such as war, plagues, and famine.[3] The belief systems of the Gnostics threatened the power of the Catholic church. Some have suggested the Catholic church fabricated tales of sexualized, violent rituals as a means to persecute its adversaries.

Most Gnostic sects rejected the Ten Commandments of Moses because they were given to him by the inferior God of the Old Testament. Gnostic sects developed their own standards of morality. Some suggest that these early Gnostics believed that bringing a child into this world of darkness was a sin. The Gnostics were speculated to have believed that because this world was ruled by the God of the Old Testament, giving birth to a child was doing a grave injustice to the child's spirit, who longed to be with the Supreme Unknown God. Birth into this world of evil was a cruel injustice to the soul. Some Gnostic sects were also thought to have worshiped their own semen and menstrual blood because both contained the life-giving force.[4] For more detailed information on Gnostic beliefs, please refer to the books listed in Resources.

In the Middle Ages, some secret societies and fraternal organizations were accused by the Catholic church of practicing a violent, sexualized mass. In the thirteenth century, the Cathars were accused of practicing devil worship, human sacrifice, incest, homosexuality, and celebrating the "Black Mass." According to Michael Howard, author of *The Occult Conspiracy,* the accusations of practicing a Black Mass were based on the Cathar practice of engaging in a love feast, a rite they had inherited from the pagan mysteries. The Catholic church launched a crusade and killed thousands of members of the order.[5]

In the fourteenth century, the Knights Templar were also accused by the church of denying the tenets of the Christian faith, spitting and urinating on the cross, worshiping a skull and anointing it with the blood or the fat of unbaptized babies. According to Howard, during confessions Templars said the ceremonies took place at night in candle-lit chapels. They said they were forced to renounce their Christian faith as a sign of their loyalty to the Order, and they were asked to spit, urinate, or trample on the cross. Unfortunately, the torture and blackmail used by the church to obtain confessions makes it difficult to separate fact from fiction in regard to the accusations.[6]

The Illuminati

In the eighteenth century, another secret society openly dedicated itself to the destruction of monarchies and standardized religion. The group's primary aim was to establish a government and religion that represented the people. The name of this group was the Illuminati. Because the Illuminati were known subversives, the group had to go into hiding. Some suggest members of the Illuminati infiltrated mainstream secret societies and fraternal organizations, including Freemasonry, as an attempt to achieve their political and spiritual aims.[7]

The Illuminati are the most widely recognized secret society associated with satanism, although the Illuminati were not satanists and did not worship the devil to gain personal power. Illuminist philosophies were based on dualism. According to Carl Raschke, university professor, researcher on satanism, and author of *Painted Black*:

> The point to bear in mind is that Illuminism aimed from its outset to accomplish what alchemists and occultists have called the "great work" as a social and political undertaking. The "magical" objective of the Illuminati was abolition of a millennium of feudalism together with the creation of a universal, utopian society, that knitted together all humankind. At the same time, Illuminist politics were fired by a self-conscious worship of the deepest and most compelling instinctual urgings of the human organism. Only the reign of the violent and repressed would be sufficient to liberate humanity from the tyranny of religion, law, and class domination . . . The use of a naked woman as an altar (during the so-called Black Mass), and the substitution of fecal matter for the consecrated host, were not simply blasphemy. They were direct expressions of the dualistic idea that the horrible and the glorious, the shadowy and the resplendent, must be exhibited together as the supreme revelation of "secret knowledge."[8]

This "secret knowledge" is probably the same revelation author Kurt Seligmann describes in *The History of Magic and the Occult*:

> The best minds of the West were influenced by a higher type of magic. The investigators of nature followed for centuries the path trodden before them by ancient philosophers and magi. They believed that in magical wisdom lay the secret of the world's harmony. The religions of the West have admitted that Satan's revolt split the universe, that he infests the world of matter, and that the ever-tempted believer may gain lasting felicity only after

death. The magical systems of the old did not admit disharmony. They encircled the totality of being, good and evil, life and death, the visible and the invisible. All is contained in All. And All in One. The supernatural is not separate from the world of matter, but is infused in every object. Good and Evil sprang from the same source; both obey the same law.[9]

The "secret knowledge" is most likely a revelation of the source of both good and evil. In order to find the source, some secret societies and fraternal organizations might have required members to engage in acts described as evil and acts described as good. Once initiates found the source of their own behavior, it might have been believed that members then acted from their true spiritual natures.

A theme common to most secret societies accused of violent masses is a global ambition to unite the world under the principles of peace and world harmony. The groups did not accept traditional Christianity as the vehicle of peace. They believed that Christianity, as dictated by the Catholic church, hindered human beings from their true spiritual nature. The groups believed that understanding God must be an active experience accomplished through a variety of spiritual practices and revelations that are taught at each stage of the group's initiation rites.

As the Catholic church became more corrupt—for example, charging people money to receive forgiveness for their sins—secret societies and fraternal organizations might have seemed like an attractive alternative to meet people's spiritual needs. The secret societies' noble aims of forming worldwide peace appealed to the learned men of the past. Another attraction was the occult practice of worshiping the Feminine Principle in the form of the Goddess. For many, the worship of the Goddess filled the void left within traditional Christianity, which refers to God as a masculine entity. The groups tended to attract the intelligent elite who were unhappy with the status quo.[10]

Freemasonry

Historically, certain secret societies and fraternal organizations were accused of practicing a violent, sexualized mass. Survivors in this study also reported a relationship between perpetrator involvement in secret societies and the practice of ritual abuse. Sixty-seven percent of the survivors said their ritual abuse perpetrators were members of secret societies or fraternal organizations. Thirty-three percent said perpetrating family members were Masons. Survivors also reported a variety of other secret societies in which their fathers were members. Since a number of survivors in this study reported their perpetrators were Masons, this section describes Masonry in detail.

Masonry is an extensive examination of the nature of God. Albert Pike's *Morals and Dogma of the Ancient and Accepted Scottish Rite of Freemasonry,* an 861-page book to be studied by Masons of the highest degrees, is an array of historical, mythological, philosophical, and logical examinations of God. The book is difficult to read because Pike continually refers to mythological gods and goddesses of other cultures. Pike attempts to use logic and reason to convey to the reader the existence of a Universal God that could unite all people.

Here Pike reveals to the reader the doctrine of Freemasonry:

> While all these faiths assert their claims to the exclusive possession of Truth, Masonry inculcates its old doctrine, and no more: ... That God is ONE; that HIS THOUGHT uttered in His WORD, created the Universe, and preserves it by those Eternal Laws which are the expression of that Thought; that the Soul of Man, breathed into him by God, is immortal as His Thoughts are; that he is free to do evil or to choose good, responsible for his acts and punishable for his sins: that all evil and wrong and suffering are but temporary, the discords of one great Harmony, and that in His good time they will lead by infinite modulations to the great, harmonic final chord and cadence of Truth, Love, Peace, and Happiness, that will ring forever and ever under the Arches of Heaven, among all the Stars and Worlds, and in all souls of men and Angels.[11]

In the closing paragraphs of the book, Pike describes how the Great Harmony is supposed to happen.

>And as in each Triangle of Perfection, one is three and
>three are one, so man is one, though of a double nature; and
>he attains the purposes of his being only when the two
>natures that are in him are in just equilibrium . . .[12]

The two natures Pike talks about are humankind's appetite for pleasure tamed by a moral sense. If people learn to balance both, he
says, they are able to live under a free government based on liberty
while the people still obey the law.

The Masons are one of the most powerful and influential
organizations in the world. A number of books have been written on
the historical and present power of the Masons. Masonic dreams of
freedom and liberty were principles that influenced the founding of
the United States. Howard, author of *The Occult Conspiracy*, notes
that fifty of the fifty-six signers of the Declaration of Independence
were Masons. George Washington and John Adams were both high-
ranking Masons. Some suggest there is side of history that reveals
how secret societies and fraternal organizations have been responsible for the Protestant Reformation, the founding of the United States
of America, the Declaration of Independence, and the two World
Wars.[13]

Aleister Crowley

Aleister Crowley, a well-known British occultist at the turn of the
century, was also a high-ranking Mason. Publicly, Crowley was
believed to be a satanist interested in the darker side of the occult.
He was well known for his participation in sexualized masses,
which he referred to as Gnostic Masses.[14]

Crowley also envisioned a world based on the principles of
world peace and harmony. After finishing his *Book of Lies*, Crowley
was approached by a fraternal organization that told him he had
found the "supreme secret" and that he was now obligated in regard
to it. Crowley said he knew no such secret, but the leaders of the
order turned to a page in the *Book of Lies* and told him he had
printed it in clearest language.[15] The passage that they referred to is
most likely the only passage that contradicts the theme of the book.
In the closing chapter, Crowley states:

Behold! I have lived many years, and I have travelled in every land that is under the dominion of the Sun, and I have sailed the seas from pole to pole. Now do I lift up my voice and testify that all is vanity on earth, except for the love of a good woman, and that woman LAYLAH. And I testify that in heaven all is vanity (for I have journeyed oft, and sojourned oft, in every heaven), except the love of Our Lady Babylon . . . And at the End is She that was Laylah, and Babylon, and Nuit, being . . .[16]

Laylah was a woman Crowley loved, and he referred to her in his book on numerous occasions. He stated in the closing of the book that all in life is vanity except love. His comment, which accompanies the chapter, reads:

This chapter is a sort of final Confession of Faith. It is the unification of all symbols and all planes. The End is inexpressible.[17]

After Crowley was aware of the "supreme secret," he stated in the book *The Confessions of Aleister Crowley:*

I understood I held in my hands the key to the future progress of humanity . . .[18]

Crowley also wrote *The Book of the Law,* a text that is believed by some occultists to be the foundation for the formation of a religion to unite all people. The theme of love is a primary part of the book. Part I of the book is the voice of the goddess Nuit, who prepares the world for her marriage with her consort Hadit. Her rituals are not to be celebrated with violence.

At all my meetings with you shall the priestess say—and her eyes shall burn with desire as she stands bare rejoicing in my secret temple—To me! To me! calling forth the flame of the hearts of all in her love-chant. Sing rapturous love song unto me! Burn to me perfumes! Wear to me jewels! Drink to me, for I love you! I love you![19]

Part II of the book is the voice of Hadit, the consort of Nuit. He is hidden from the goddess. The final part of the book is the voice of the God of War of Vengeance. The voice of this God is the voice of violence and power. In Part III of *The Book of the Law,* Crowley makes references to the violent, sexualized mass variously described throughout history.

> Worship me with fire & blood; worship me with swords & spears. Let the woman be girt with a sword before me: let blood flow to my name. Trample down the Heathen; be upon them, o warrior, I will give you their flesh to eat! Sacrifice cattle, little and big: after a child . . . For perfume mix meal & honey & thick leavings of red wine: then oil of Abramelin and olive oil, and afterward soften & smooth down with rich fresh blood. The best blood is of the moon, monthly; then the fresh blood of a child, or dropping from the host of heaven; then of enemies; then of the priest or of the worshippers; last of some beast, no matter what. This burn: of this and make cakes & eat unto me.[20]

Crowley was hired by powerful Masons to standardize worldwide Masonic practices. At the time, there was a great deal of disagreement among Masonic lodges. Crowley notes:

> Faced with these, and similar difficulties, I gladly accepted the task laid upon me by the most intelligent freemasons of the world, united as they were by their sincerity, understanding and good will, though divided by sectarian squabbles about jurisdiction.[21]

Crowley's ideas were never adopted by the Masons because the men who had hired Crowley were unable to take the action necessary to implement the changes.[22]

Initiation Rites of Freemasonry

A primary part of Masonry is the participation in dramatic "skits" or rituals that are supposed to connect members to a higher spiritual reality. For example, playing the part of an important historical or mythological figure during a ritual is supposed to connect the initiate to the spiritual significance of the legend or tale. In the book

The Deadly Deception, author Jim Shaw, an ex-member of the Masons, describes initiation rites in which group members acted out skits:

> Dressed in long, black, hooded robes, we marched in single file, with only our faces partly showing, and took our seats[23]... We then swore true allegiance to the Supreme council of the 33rd Degree above all other allegiances... One of the Conductors then handed the "candidate" a human skull, upside down, with wine in it.[24]

When Shaw was granted the degree of Master Mason, he was assaulted during a ritual in which he was supposed to play the part of Hiram Abiff, architect of Solomon's Temple.

> Jubela then got even more violent, demanding the secret word, right then! Again speaking for me, the Senior Deacon said, "Craftsman, I cannot and will not give them" upon which Jubela struck a blow across my throat with the 24-inch gauge. It hurt and startled me...[25]

During initiation rites as a Shriner (one of the highest branches of Freemasonry), Shaw witnessed vulgarities during rituals.

> At one point we were placed in a large, mesh cage, and one of the Shriners climbed on top of it. He exposed a very convincing rubber penis which was connected to a water bag concealed in his clothing and hosed down all of us in the cage to the delighted howls of the spectators.[26]

Shaw said when he received his highest degree in Masonry, he was flown to Washington, D.C. There, behind closed doors, he met high-ranking Masons, including a Scandinavian king, two ex-presidents of the United States, and two internationally prominent clergymen.[27]

Shaw and other Masons are silenced about the power and practices of Masons by the threats made to them in their first degrees of Masonry. Shaw stated:

> As it [the oath] progressed I realized that I was swearing to protect the secrets of the Lodge. Then I heard myself

saying that I was "binding myself under no less penalty than that of having my throat cut from ear to ear, my tongue torn out by its roots, and buried in the sands of the sea . . . if I should ever willingly, knowingly, or unlawfully violate this, my Entered Apprentice Oath, so help me God and keep me steadfast."[28]

In her master's thesis on ritual abuse, Ann-Marie Germain recalls a number of conversations she had with her father about Masonry. Ann-Marie is a ritual abuse survivor and her father, a 32nd-degree Mason and a Shriner (deceased), was one of her perpetrators. When Ann-Marie was seven, her father moved away from her hometown in an attempt, she believes, to flee from the Masons. In her dissertation, Germain recalls conversations she had with her father about Masonry. Miss Germain was amnesic of the ritual abuse when the following conversations occurred:

ME: Daddy, did you see the newspaper article about plans to put up a big new building on the Masonic Temple property?

HIM: It's the Sarasota Lodge, not Temple, Ann.

ME: Well, whatever it's called. It doesn't matter.

HIM: Yes, it does matter. I wanted us to move to Sarasota instead of Clearwater because there wasn't any Temple here and it wasn't likely there would be one. There weren't enough Masons here with the money to build one. Now I'm afraid they might build a Temple on the Lodge property. (said with seriousness and real fear)

ME: Why are you afraid of it? I thought you'd be glad, why didn't you want to move where there was a Temple?

HIM: They do things in Temples that can't be done in a Lodge. (He looked away from me, out the window as he spoke, with a hard, closed face.)

ME: What's wrong with that? What kind of things?

HIM: I can't tell you Ann! (exasperated with my probing) They do bad things and it's all kept secret.[29]

Ann-Marie's father did not want her to join the Eastern Star, an organization for the wives of Masons. Ann-Marie notes a conversation she had with her father on the topic.

ME: Do you know if the wives of any of your friends at Shriners belong to Eastern Star?

HIM: No. Why?

ME: I'd like to learn about them. I might want to join.

HIM: No! Don't go there. It's not a good group. It's dangerous for you to go there. (His serious, warning tone of voice frightened me off. I sensed he really meant it, but he wouldn't tell me why.)[30]

As her father grew older, he spoke to Ann-Marie about his fear of going to Hell.

ME: What's wrong Daddy?

HIM: I'm afraid to die. I'm afraid I won't go to heaven.

ME: But you're a Christian.

HIM: You don't understand. (A sentence that he said to me many times in those years)

ME: You told me about being saved by Billy Sunday when you were just a boy. And you've been a Deacon at the church all these years. (pause)

HIM: That doesn't matter. The Masons taught one thing and the Christians another, and I believed the Masons. I was convinced. Even the preacher was part of the Masons. Now, I don't know what to think, and I'm afraid I'm going to Hell. I've done some terrible things.

ME: If you're sorry, you can ask God to forgive you and He will.

HIM: I doubt it.

ME: It says in the Bible that He will forgive if we repent and ask for forgiveness in Jesus' name.

HIM: I know, Ann. But that won't work for me.[31]

Ann-Marie's father expressed on a few occasions remorse for acts she could not remember.

ME: What's wrong Daddy?

HIM: I'm sorry, Ann. I'm really sorry. I didn't know. I didn't realize how much harm was being done.

ME: Sorry for what?

HIM: You really don't remember, do you?

ME: Remember what?

HIM: I can't tell you. If you don't remember, I can't tell you. It might do more harm than good.

ME: Well, I don't know what to say because I don't know what you're talking about.

HIM: I know it. That's all right. At least I am leaving an inheritance, a house, and $50,000. I wish it were more, but it's all I can do. It'll help some. It's not enough, but it's a pretty good amount. A lot better than nothing.

(Later)

HIM: I need you to forgive me.

ME: (I didn't understand, but remembered our talk about his fear of Hell so I responded to that.) If you ask God to forgive you, you'll be forgiven.

HIM: No. I need *you* to forgive me. (His voice was very quiet, and pleading.)

ME: For what?

HIM: (He paused, tears coming to his eyes.) I can't tell you.

ME: (I paused too, wanting to console him, watching him wipe his tears. I tried to reassure him.) Well, it doesn't matter if I forgive you, it's God's forgiveness that counts.

HIM: I don't think God will forgive me. I'm resigned to that. What I did was too bad. But I'd feel better if I could know that you forgave me.

ME: (I was near tears myself in compassion for his pain.) I'd forgive you if I could, if I knew what it was about, Daddy.

HIM: Do you mean that?

ME: Yes. If you didn't know, like you said, if you didn't realize you were doing harm, I wouldn't hold it against you. I can see you're really sorry. (There was relief on his face as he searched my face and saw that I meant what I said.)[32]

THE CULT NETWORK

Sixty-seven percent of the survivors in this study said they were abused by more than one cult group. This illustrates how many cults that ritually abuse children share their victims and communicate with one another. Most survivors said their perpetrators were involved in the distribution and trading of child pornography. Some survivors said their abusers were involved in drug trafficking and organized crime. Some survivors say there is a network of violent cults that operate in a businesslike fashion similar to the organized crime network and are involved in ritual abuse, organized crime, and child pornography.

Prevalence and Power

Cults that ritually abuse children are found all over the world. Survivors in this study were abused in forty-five of the fifty United States. Survivors also said they were abused in Scotland, England, Germany, Mexico, South America, and Canada (see Table 6.1).

Survivors were abused out of doors, in people's homes, and in churches (see Table 6.2). The abusers had access to public buildings. The occupations of the abusers, as noted in the previous chapter, allow them access to these buildings.

Why Don't They Get Caught?

Violent cults take precautions to protect themselves. Rituals usually take place late at night, while most people are sleeping. Programming is designed to silence members, often by causing amnesia in the victims. The cults are cautious about where they perform rituals. Often rituals are performed in buildings owned by members, in basements or in rooms with no windows. If rituals are performed

Table 6.1   States in Which Survivors Were
Ritually Abused

California	37%	Vermont	4%
New York	15%	Wisconsin	4%
Washington	12%	Wyoming	4%
Michigan	10%	Connecticut	2%
Illinois	8%	Delaware	2%
Arizona	6%	Georgia	2%
Indiana	6%	Idaho	2%
Louisiana	6%	Kansas	2%
Maryland	6%	Kentucky	2%
New Jersey	6%	Minnesota	2%
Ohio	6%	Mississippi	2%
Tennessee	6%	Montana	2%
Arkansas	4%	Nebraska	2%
Colorado	4%	New Hampshire	2%
Florida	4%	New Mexico	2%
Maine	4%	North Carolina	2%
Massachusetts	4%	Pennsylvania	2%
Nevada	4%	Utah	2%
Oregon	4%	Virginia	2%
Pennsylvania	4%	Washington, D.C.	2%
Texas	4%	West Virginia	2%

outside, cults make sure they are in remote areas and scouts patrol the site to ensure that onlookers are not present. Human sacrifices are usually eaten or burned.

If a violent cult is caught practicing such rituals, it is difficult to prosecute members specifically for ritual abuse–related crimes. The cases are tried simply on molestation charges, pornography charges, or organized crime charges while ignoring the ritual-related accusations of the victims.

Table 6.2   Specific Locations at Which the Ritual
Abuse Occurred

Outside (woods, fields, etc.)	65%	School (nursery–high)	19%
Church (usually the basement)	50%	Theater/Film studio	12%
		Warehouse	10%
Home other than parents'	42%	Medical building	8%
Farms, ranches, barns	33%	Funeral home	6%
Parents' home	29%	Beach	6%
Graveyard	25%		

Other Locations Mentioned by Survivors

Abandoned building	My workplace
Boat	My father's workplace
Bomb shelter	Old hotel
Businesses	Parks
Carnival	Police vehicles
Community meeting center	Restaurant
Crematorium	Salt mines
Factory	Scottish Rite Temple
Main house on secluded rural estate	Slaughterhouse
Masonic Lodge	Summer camp
Mausoleum	Steel mill
Military base	Vacant apartments
Museum	

Ritual abuse–related crime, especially satanic ritual abuse, has for many years been a taboo topic among law enforcement professionals. Politically, it is very unpopular for police commissioners or public officials to acknowledge that ritual abuse is a problem in their community.

Most people don't hear about ritual abuse because they don't want to. In the past, many reputable newspapers, television stations, and publishing houses were unwilling to publish on the topic because the public was unwilling to believe that ritual abuse happens. Most people have a difficult time accepting that atrocities are being committed on a large scale. The American public, for example, didn't want to know about the millions of Jews being killed in Germany prior to WWII. If we had acknowledged that Jews were being tortured and killed in concentration camps, morally we would have felt obligated to take action.

The same is true regarding ritual abuse. When we acknowledge that it is happening, we feel compelled to make it stop. However, it is the inability to believe ritual abuse survivors that is the greatest factor protecting violent cults. Only when we acknowledge that ritual abuse happens—and these survivors who are speaking out receive our support and compassion rather than our interrogations and judgment—will more survivors come forward. As it stands now, ritual abuse survivors who have the courage to remember the abuse and talk about it often face disbelief and insensitivity.

NOTES

1. *The New Merriam-Webster Dictionary* (Springfield, MA: Merriam-Webster, 1989), 440.

2. Sally Hill, M.S.W., and Jean Goodwin, M.D., M.P.H., "Satanism: Similarities Between Patient Accounts and Preinquisition Historical Sources," *Dissociation: Progress in Dissociative Disorders* 2, no. 1 (1989): 39–42.

3. Benjamin Walker, *Gnosticism: Its History and Influence* (Wellingborough, Northamptonshire, UK: Crucible, 1989), 41–44.

4. Walker, *Gnosticism,* 120, 131.

5. Michael Howard, *The Occult Conspiracy* (Rochester, VT: Destiny Books, 1989), 26.

6. Howard, *The Occult Conspiracy,* 37.

7. Howard, *The Occult Conspiracy,* 62.

8. Carl Raschke, *Painted Black* (San Francisco: HarperSanFrancisco, 1990), 87.

9. Kurt Seligmann, *The History of Magic and the Occult* (New York: Harmony Books, 1975), 321.

10. Raschke, *Painted Black,* 83.

11. Albert Pike, *Morals and Dogma of the Ancient and Accepted Scottish Rite of Freemasonry* (Washington, D.C.: House of the Temple, 1966; originally published in 1871), 577.

12. Pike, *Morals and Dogma,* 861.

13. Howard, *The Occult Conspiracy,* 82.

14. Aleister Crowley, *The Confessions of Aleister Crowley,* edited by John Symonds and Kenneth Grant (London: Arkana, 1979), 13 (footnote).

15. Crowley, *Confessions,* 710.

16. Aleister Crowley, *The Book of Lies* (York Beach, ME: Samuel Weiser, 1988), 190.

17. Crowley, *The Book of Lies,* 191.

18. Crowley, *Confessions,* 710.

19. Aleister Crowley, *The Law Is for All: An Extenuation of The Book of Law* (Las Vegas, NV: The Falcon Press, 1988), 50–51.

20. Crowley, *The Law Is for All,* 58–60.

21. Crowley, *Confessions,* 700.

22. Crowley, *Confessions,* 707.

23. Jim Shaw and Tom McKenney, *The Deadly Deception* (Lafayette, LA: Huntington House, 1988), 106.

24. Shaw and McKenney, *The Deadly Deception,* 104.

25. Shaw and McKenney, *The Deadly Deception,* 49–50.

26. Shaw and McKenney, *The Deadly Deception,* 75.

27. Shaw and McKenney, *The Deadly Deception,* 104.

28. Shaw and McKenney, *The Deadly Deception,* 26.

29. Ann-Marie Germain, *Ritual Abuse: Its Effects and the Process of Recovery Using Self-help Methods and Resources, and Focusing on the Spiritual Aspect of Damage and Recovery* (Carbondale, IL: Southern Illinois University at Carbondale, 1992), 227. Master's thesis; unpublished.

30. Germain, *Ritual Abuse,* 225–26.

31. Germain, *Ritual Abuse,* 229.

32. Germain, *Ritual Abuse,* 230.

Chapter 7

Getting Out

This chapter was difficult to write because I didn't want to scare anyone. After thinking it over, I decided I had to tell people all that I know in order to give survivors the tools they need to protect themselves from their abusers.

Not surprisingly, like most destructive cults, violent cults try to control almost every aspect of their members' lives. When ritual abuse survivors have the courage to remember adult ritual abuse, they remember what seems to be willing participation in these violent rituals. They usually remember that loved ones and close family members are involved in the cult. When survivors have these memories, they are overcome with fear and disbelief.

I don't want survivors to be overcome with panic. I want them to believe their personalities, who want to protect them from further victimization. Based on my own experience, here are some suggestions to help survivors get through these difficult times.

1. *Don't let fear consume you. Tell your personalities that you must control your fear, until you are safe. If you become overwhelmed with your fear, you won't be able to effectively protect yourself. You might become paralyzed and give up.*

2. *Allow your personalities to remember information about the current ritual abuse memories without the physical sensations or emotions. From these memories, you must make decisions about how to protect yourself from further victimization.*

3. *Don't be surprised if you remember close friends and family members who are involved in the ritual abuse. If you do remember their involvement, you might be overwhelmed with*

grief from potentially losing a relationship with them. Although you must limit contact with loved ones who are still involved in the cult, you can still love them and have them in your life. In order to protect yourself, you must exercise certain precautions, but you may find that your loved ones are in the same boat that you are. They are also victims waiting for change.

4. *It is in your friends' best interest that you break free. Once you're free, the cult can no longer force them to hurt you. You show loved ones that it's not hopeless. There is a way out.*

5. *Don't alienate your personalities who seem to be willing participants in the cults. It is important to remember your own victimization. If you befriend these cult personalities, they can help you break free. If you alienate them or disbelieve them, they will turn to the cult for support.*

6. *You don't always have to be aware of the behaviors of these cult personalities in order for them to help you. If you have their respect, they can slowly manipulate their abusers, loosening their ties to the cult. They can plan their escape, while you learn to protect yourself from victimization.*

Remember:

1. *Cults don't usually kill members who were ritually abused as children. In their eyes, such people are an investment, and they will wait indefinitely to collect on their investment.*

2. *In time they will stop pursuing you because it reminds them that they are losing. In an arrogant stance, they will leave you alone, still believing you will come back eventually.*

3. *As you are breaking free, if you have personalities that are still returning to the cult, they will be reprogrammed and tortured. This will make you especially fearful and confused. At this point, make the break as soon as possible. Keep control of your fear, and manipulate your abusers however you have to in order to make yourself safe.*

4. *You don't have to punish yourself for searching for freedom.*

5. *Each day your mind will become clearer, and you will find they have less control over your life. Someday you will truly know the meaning of the word freedom.*

HOW LENGTH OF ABUSE INFLUENCES ABILITY
TO LEAVE

The length of time that survivors were abused generally determines whether they will be able to get out of the cult before memories of the abuse surface as an adult. A survivor who was abused outside of the home only for a short duration of time—who was not forced to participate for the first eighteen years of life—has some freedom from the cult brainwashing. A survivor who was raised from infancy to adulthood in a cult, however, faces a different situation because the cult controlled almost every aspect of this person's life. Survivors who grew up in cults have the most difficult time ever breaking free.

Abuse for a Short Duration of Time
During Childhood

Some children are ritually abused in day-care centers for two or three years, or by only one family member for a short duration of time. These children spend most of their lives away from the cult learning a different way of life. Although the programming and pain of the ritual abuse remains hidden in their minds, they still develop relationships with noncult members. The cult doesn't control every aspect of their lives.

Because it is short, the programming of these children is less effective than the programming of children raised in cults. However, if they were never allowed to confront and have comforted the pain from the abuse during childhood, as adults they may feel pulled to violent groups to relive the trauma of their own abuse. They may join an occult organization only to find themselves later stuck in a cult that ritually abuses children, still unaware of their own ritual abuse histories. Even though the cults have less overt control of these survivors than survivors who were raised in cults, their lives are still greatly affected by the abuse.

Children abused for a short duration of time are usually programmed during torture to return to the cult at a specific age later in life, and to remain amnesic of their cult involvement. Survivors who get pulled into cults in this way end up being trapped in a cult due to their amnesia.

Children Ritually Abused Throughout Their
Entire Childhoods

Some children are abused by either one or both of their parents from infancy until they are able to leave home. Usually, this means they are abused for the first eighteen years of their lives. If no one steps in to protect them from the abusers, by the time survivors are old enough to move away, the group already has complete control of their lives through amnesia and intensive programming.

The cults do not want to lose their highly programmed members. If one of these members tries to leave the group, cults will go out of their way to bring the member back. These survivors not only have to worry about their brainwashed personalities returning to the cult, but they also have to worry about the group physically forcing them to return. Sometimes it seems easier to these survivors to remain amnesic of their cult involvement and to stay in denial about the abuse. Staying in denial keeps them from feeling the intense anxiety and fear of knowing how difficult it is to get away.

If a survivor raised in a violent cult tries to break free, she will face increasing difficulty when she tries to get out of the group, depending on how involved her parents were in the cults. Just as some people are more involved in politics than others, some parents are more involved in the cults than others. Most of the families who are deeply involved in the cults have multigenerational involvement— the parents are also survivors of ritual abuse. Many of these families have held specific roles in the cults for centuries. The cults are very concerned with maintaining the lineage of these families, and if a survivor from a highly involved family tries to leave, then the cults will take any action necessary to bring the survivor back. Children born into these highly involved families will have the most difficult time breaking free.

Amnesia is the most powerful weapon these cults use to control their members. Sometimes survivors remember their childhood ritual abuse only to realize later, in their process of healing, that they are still being abused in cults today. Some survivors can believe they are out of the cults as an adult, only to later realize they had certain personalities who never left the group. When they remember the abuse as adults, sometimes they are fearful of being pulled back into a cult without their knowledge. This is possible if survivors are amnesic of certain experiences of their alter personalities.

HOW CULTS TRY TO KEEP MEMBERS

Cults put a lot of time into programming members, so it's not surprising that they would try their best to retain these members. They use various methods to this end, including accessing personalities, reprogramming, threats, infiltration of survivor resources, and the influence of friends and family members.

Accessing

Part of programming is designed to teach survivors specific symbols, words, or sounds that "trigger" them to change personalities. The survivors are taught these triggers while pain is being inflicted, when their minds are the most easily influenced. If amnesic members do not willingly return to the cult, the cult will access alter personalities using these trigger words. Triggering personalities makes survivors unaware of their personality switches. When a survivor switches to a triggered alter personality, the cult is able to have complete control of the survivor's behavior without the survivor's daily personalities being aware of the personality switch. The daily life personalities are amnesic of the alter personalities' experiences.

These triggered alter personalities are at the mercy of the cult. They are the tortured personalities who feel all of the survivors' pain. They feel the weakness the strong personalities shook off when they were able to make a break from the cult. These personalities are like zombies. Triggered personalities obey cult orders because they are afraid of being hurt. If other personalities are able to protect them from harm, they slowly are able to develop the strength to say no to accessing triggers. Personalities in the day-to-day life must take precautions to protect the vulnerable personalities from being accessed and physically harmed. This is one of the most difficult parts of getting away from the cult. Often the day-to-day personalities do not want to know the extent of their ritual abuse histories. Only when survivors listen to their personalities and break the amnesia are they able to protect themselves.

Even though there is a set of tortured personalities in most survivors who are as vulnerable to the cult as children, there are also personalities in most multiple systems who are every bit as strong as the abusers. These personalities can take action to protect the other personalities from harm. They can play whatever games they have to play with the abusers to move themselves to a place where they are able to get out.

Reprogramming

If a survivor has been talking about the ritual abuse or contemplating leaving the group, and then is accessed, she will be reprogrammed. Reprogramming, like the original programming, also usually takes place during extensive torture sessions. When survivors are reprogrammed, they are told the same lies they were told in their childhood: That they are unlovable, that they are evil, and that they do not belong in the world. The context of the lies is updated to fit their current life situations. The cults tell the survivors that the people they love really hate them. They say whatever they have to say to make survivors feel weak and powerless against the group.

Threats

Abusers sometimes are able to control survivors with threats. Some survivors return to the cult when they are afraid their loved ones will be hurt. Only when survivors break free of the cult and pave the ground for others to follow are loved ones truly given an opportunity to be protected and free. They are given an example that getting out is possible and the situation is not hopeless.

Infiltration of Resources for Ritual Abuse Survivors

Abusers are able to stop survivors from getting out by placing their own members in roles as ritual abuse recovery advocates. Cult members who are therapists are programmed to take on ritual abuse clients. In this way, the cult can control what memories survivors are allowed to recall. This keeps the important cult secrets protected. Sometimes cults infiltrate organizations for ritual abuse survivors to control the type of information that is given to recovering survivors.

In general, cult therapists and cult organizations teach the following philosophy to keep members trapped in cults. "It's okay to remember your own childhood ritual abuse, but don't remember any current cult involvement." Or they teach that people who are being ritually abused as adults are "evil" or less strong than other survivors of ritual abuse. In the eyes of the cults, if survivors only remember their childhood ritual abuse, then the cults aren't threatened. If survivors remember abuse that is happening today, however, then the cults are in danger of losing members or of having some of their current operations placed in jeopardy.

Using Friends and Family from the Cult to Pull the Survivor Back In

Cult members in abusive situations develop intimate bonds with one another, similar to the bonds developed between war veterans. The survivor doesn't want to lose her closest friends, yet these friends may be the people keeping her in the cult. In order to protect herself, she would have to greatly limit her contact with the people she is closest to in the world.

It's not surprising, then, that when a survivor attempts to leave the group, the cult often uses the person's cult friends to pull her back in. Even though a friend who does the accessing is acting on orders it is very difficult for survivors' daily-life personalities to acknowledge that their friends may be pulling them back into the cult. This makes such a tactic extremely effective.

Sometimes old family or friends call survivors when they are trying to get out to remind survivors they are bonded to people inside of the cult. The message to the survivor is that "the cult is your home" and that cult people "are your family." It is very painful for survivors who are trying to leave the cult to be reminded that they are leaving people they really care about, only to face a world that doesn't seem to accept them. Sometimes these phone calls stir up old feelings of attachment to the cult and are enough to keep survivors from leaving the group.

Married to a Cult Member

If a survivor is married to a cult member, the chances of getting out of the group are next to impossible. Both spouses must decide between themselves, in their daily lives and in their cult lives, to get out of the group. They must commit to each other—giving their ultimate loyalty to themselves, not to the cult. Even when spouses are able to make this commitment, the cult will try to drive a wedge between them by trying to convince one spouse that the other is lying. If the spouse believes the cult and becomes loyal to the group again, neither spouse can get out. The loyal spouse will continue to access the spouse who wants to get free until neither trusts the other. Once more, the cult has power over their relationship and their futures. In these cases, in order for survivors to get out, they must separate from their spouses for their own protection.

HOW TO PROTECT YOURSELF FROM THE CULT

Despite what the cult tells them, it is possible for survivors to protect themselves from the cult. Here are some ways that work.

Move Away

Most cults that ritually abuse children seem to be organized in a structured network similar to the organized crime network. When a survivor who is raised in a local cult moves to another city or state, the survivor will be programmed prior to the move to contact cult members in the new town. For example, survivors may be programmed to meet cult contacts in support groups, or survivors might be told to call "old Aunt Mary," a cult member who will set them up with a cult in the new city. All of this programming to reconnect with a new cult is isolated to cult personalities. The survivors' daily personalities only feel the results of the programming as an ache or a loneliness to find someone to be close to. Consciously, survivors are not aware that joining a support group or calling a family member will pull them back into a cult.

For most survivors, simply moving to another city is not a solution for breaking free from the group. However, moving is beneficial. Often the cults that raised an individual survivor have a greater investment in the child staying in the group than another group that barely knows the survivor. The cult in a different city won't try as hard as the survivor's home group to pull her back in.

Live in a Safe Environment

In order to get out of the group, survivors must live in a safe environment. They must take extra precautions to assure that the cult is not able to send a person over to their house to access them in the middle of the night. Fortunately, in most cases this is relatively easy. Usually, cults only break into survivors' homes in ways that would look like burglaries to the police. If survivors keep their homes safe from ordinary prowlers, then cult members usually won't break into their homes.

Have Selective Contact with People in Isolated Environments

Often cults are unable to effectively access survivors who are trying to get out until they are alone. If the cult attempts to access a survivor at a public restaurant, then the personalities vulnerable to accessing are not physically threatened, and they can say no. If the survivor is alone with another cult member at her house, then vulnerable personalities might be physically forced to do something they don't want to do. If survivors carefully select who they are alone with in nonpublic places, they can often avoid being accessed by the cult.

Listening to Personalities

Survivors must listen closely to their personalities. If a personality says someone is not safe, then the entire system must listen if they want to protect the system as a whole. Sometimes it is very painful for daily personalities to listen to other personalities who are knowledgeable about their cult lives. Cult people are attracted to cult people, just as all people with common experiences are attracted to one another. It is quite likely that many of the survivor's closest friends are also cult members. Limiting contact with these friends can be extremely painful. However, it is less painful to limit these friendships than it is for a survivor to remain controlled by the cult for the rest of her life.

It is important to remember that daily-life personalities are not the personalities who know about the ritual abuse. They don't know who in their lives may be cult members. They do not know how the cult works. It is the personalities that survivors are amnesic of that have these answers.

Survivors must listen to silenced personalities in order to assure the safety of the entire system. Sometimes it takes years before survivors have enough communication and cooperation in their multiple systems to effectively protect themselves from the cult. Nonetheless, it is the silenced personalities who need to be listened to if survivors want out of the cult: They know when they are in danger. They are the ones who know how to keep themselves safe.

Finding Support

Survivors who break free of the cults need a safe place where they can express their thoughts and feelings, where they don't have to censor what their personalities say. It is important for survivors to have at least one person in their lives who listens to all their ritual abuse memories, and who supports them in breaking free of the cult. If survivors don't find this necessary support, it is possible to get out, but it is an extremely painful and isolating experience.

In order to overcome the amnesia, survivors must listen to their personalities and treat them with respect. They can't do this if they are seeing a therapist who is unwilling to hear about current ritual abuse memories. It is important for ritual abuse survivors to know up front how their therapists might react to current ritual abuse memories. Survivors need to ask their therapists in what circumstances would the therapist feel obliged to report the memories to the police. Survivors need to know if they are incriminating themselves if they discuss current ritual abuse memories in therapy. It is not unusual for survivors to switch therapists because, as they remember more about the abuse, they find themselves less supported by their therapists. With so little information available to therapists about the complexities of the issues of prolonged ritual abuse, it is not unusual for therapists to unintentionally revictimize survivors. However, survivors owe it to themselves to find support in a non-revictimizing environment. If survivors want out of the cult, it is extremely important that they are heard and believed. It is essential that personalities who talk about current ritual abuse memories are not isolated or shamed by other personalities or by their therapists. If those personalities feel invalidated, they will stop talking about the current memories and continue to be victimized by the cult.

Remember: This Pain Won't Last Forever

The first years of getting out of the cult are extremely painful. Survivors must make permanent life changes in order to protect themselves, the most painful of which is the limited contact with people they are close to in the cult. There are many losses during these first few years, but the rewards are well worth it. Survivors who are finally free have an opportunity to find love and happiness.

When survivors first try to get out, they feel as if they can't trust anyone. Many survivors look around themselves, only to realize that most of the people they are close to in their lives are also cult members. In order to get out, they must limit contact with people they genuinely care about. They must always be cautious to make their homes secure at night. They may even have to leave a good job and move to a new state in order to get away from a highly possessive cult.

Survivors of ritual abuse will always have to take more precautions to protect themselves than nonsurvivors, but at some point the cults generally give up. Cults look powerless when they continue to go after someone who simply won't come back. Continuing to talk about a lost member encourages other people who are thinking about getting out to try to make an escape. Hopelessness is their strongest ploy to keep members trapped. If someone does not respond to programming for a significant length of time, it is more effective for the group to forget about that person and to wipe the slate clean, as if her or she never existed.

Realizing Why You Want to Stay

Survivors who want to break free of the group must realize and acknowledge their deepest feelings that draw them to the group. After realizing the feelings that keep them in the cult, survivors can remember the things they hated about it. They remember the threats of torture, the lies, and the manipulation. They realize that they can never be free of suffering as long as they are in the cult.

It is impossible for survivors to honestly look at their lives when the cult still has them. They can never truly face their inner feelings. They can't separate truth from lies when they are constantly threatened with violence.

WHY PEOPLE STAY IN THE CULTS

If cults are so terrible, why don't more members leave? As we have said, people remain in cults for a number of reasons, almost all of them based on fear.

Reenactment of the Abuse

Cults want to teach as many children as possible their way of viewing the world. They want to recruit as many members as possible in order to justify their own lives, which they cannot change. They say that children deserve to have a choice: a choice between the "truth" of accepting the power of pain and suffering or a "lie," living in a world that is "fake."

This philosophy usually has been the personal experience of people who were raised in cults. During violent rituals, they see the pain they are feeling inside. In the day-to-day world, they live a life pretending nothing has happened to hurt them, a life that feels "fake." Their faulty logic occurs when they believe their individual realities of suffering are the "truth" that must be taught to children.

When cult members abuse children they are really trying to recreate the scene in which they were traumatized. This enables them to feel close to the parts of themselves that dissociated during their original trauma. They can see their own pain on the victim's face, and they can also feel the victimizing power their abusers felt. In other words, they do it to feel closer to themselves.

More Painful to Leave Than to Stay

Ironically, by the time a survivor is eighteen or financially independent, and in a position to leave the group, it often seems less painful to stay. The survivor has learned to adapt. The life in the cults is put away in a neat, tidy package, covered by effective amnesia, and the day-to-day life is not as painful as it was before alter personalities were born.

The dissociation has made the survivor *unaware* of the pain, but the pain itself always remains in the body. Survivors simply identify it as resulting from something other than the ritual abuse. For example, survivors stuck in cults today may feel a deep aching and longing for something they cannot put their fingers on, or they may feel bitter, "irrational" self-loathing—"for no reason." They may feel dead inside.

Remembering the ritual abuse allows survivors to identify those feelings and realize that they are a result of the ritual abuse. By remembering, survivors can be free of the pain. Survivors who never remember will never be free of the cult and its manipulation. The aches, the longing, the feeling of internal death remain until they are able to face their pasts and get out.

Bonds with Other Group Members

People look for friends who can understand them. Children abused in cults are no different. Children who are ritually abused stick together because they can relate to one another's pain. They may have felt ashamed or exposed when they were with people who had not experienced the same violating acts. As ritual abuse survivors were growing up, they probably felt like misfits and freaks around people who had not been ritually abused.

Sometimes survivors who are trying to get free have only felt close to other ritual abuse survivors. If these other survivors are still in cults today, then leaving the group may be like leaving all

164

RITUAL ABUSE

the people they ever cared about. Even if survivors continue limited friendships with their old cult friends, a strong wedge is placed in the friendships if one survivor is trying to get out. However, until both friends are free of the group, it is difficult to have a supportive, reliable friendship without being manipulated by other group members.

Fear of Being Alone

Some survivors stuck in cults only remember their childhood ritual abuse and are unable to remember abuse that is happening today. For these survivors, it seems easier to remain amnesic of their current ritual abuse memories. Remembering the abuse in their childhood at least takes the edge off of their pain. However, if they do not actively confront their current cult involvement, they cannot make the changes that would provide them with a fulfilling life free of control. These survivors don't allow themselves to remember current ritual abuse for several reasons. They are afraid of being viewed as perpetrators and thus losing survivor support resources. They are afraid of the isolation involved with trying to protect themselves from being drawn back into the cult. Interestingly, the fear of being alone keeps many current violent cult members from leaving the group.

Brought Children into the Cult

Once a child is born to a cult member, the child is considered to belong to the cult, not to the parents. The cults force the parents to indoctrinate their children, even if they don't want to. Even if there is a time when the parents willingly participate in the abuse, the cults see that the parents are pushed past their limits until they abuse their children in ways they would never do on their own. This manipulation makes the parents hate themselves. The shame they feel about hurting their own children becomes the greatest tactic the cults use to control the parents. If the parents try to leave, the cult makes them feel ashamed and unworthy of finding a better life for the family.

It is important to remember that shame is the primary tactic used to control all cult members. The adult survivor who has a child while in the cult is probably the least likely to break free. The knowledge of bringing another person into that life of horror causes so much pain, shame, and grief that the survivor becomes paralyzed.

Alienation from Society

Society's revictimization of ritual abuse survivors keeps them tied to the cults. If survivors had a safe, supportive place to run for protection, most would go there. Unfortunately, there is no place like that for many survivors. In fact, most survivors who try to find help are revictimized. Survivors still in cults are aware of the isolation and pain faced by others who try to get out. Sometimes the pain and shame of facing non-ritual abuse survivors is too great. It may appear easier to these survivors to nurture the bonds with their old cult friends than to start relationships with people who don't seem to understand their pain.

Drawn to Their Roles and Positions in the Cult

Many survivors feel attached to their roles and positions in the cult. They are proud of their power and respect within the group. As adult members, they can control other people's behavior and do not always feel at the mercy of others. They are no longer the helpless child being victimized, and the pain of being an adult abuser is buried under layers of denial.

Sometimes survivors' own innate understanding of the world is deeply intertwined with the role they play within the group. The roles are usually very magical and mystical, bringing survivors a great feeling of connection with some higher spiritual force. During the isolation and pain of ritual abuse, survivors often reach for a powerful force outside themselves. Sometimes the strength and power they find becomes identified as an experience they can only have when they play their magical, mystical role. They believe if they stopped being in the cult and playing their role, they would lose their spiritual experiences. This connection with a higher force found in the ritual context keeps these survivors tied to the group.

Learned Not to Trust Others

Children raised in cults learned they could never rely on the love of another person. Because the cults constantly manipulate all members' feelings of love, group members who love each other often hurt one another, both intentionally and unintentionally. Any love these children did receive was about pain, not about protection and security. Nothing in life was safe for these children. Life was not fair. When life is based on these painful individual truths, people have no motivation to find a better way to live.

Rituals are designed to evoke emotion. Although the overall purpose of specific rituals may vary a great deal, all violent rituals are designed to cause pain. Spontaneous compassion during horrible events is very powerful to witness and to experience. The positive emotions that emerge after so much pain are very powerful draws for survivors to return to the cult. The positive emotions experienced in these moments of compassion and love are sometimes the only positive emotions survivors still experience.

Many violent cults are based on very old teachings. Some cults ask the question most people gave up trying to answer long ago: What is God? Our modern world puts very little emphasis on the spiritual, and some people are drawn to a cult for the simple reason that it ascribes to the belief that there is more to life than what we see around us. However, when a search for God leads people away from their own personal truth, then the search is nothing more than a manipulation of people by those in power.

Money

Money can't buy happiness; but money is what feeds us, clothes us, and puts a roof over our heads. Money can buy survivors the best psychological care, and it can also buy them time to remember the abuse without having to drag themselves to work every morning in a dissociated state.

Money is power on paper. It is a tool that can be used to ease suffering, but it can also be used to control and manipulate people depending on who has control of its distribution. When some ritual abuse survivors uncover their pasts, they collapse inside and they are in need of economic assistance. They can't put on the mask in order to go to work. The past becomes so real that the pain of covering it up is too great. At these times, the abusers, often the parents of survivors, may offer survivors money to tide them over until they can function again. Survivors are desperate when they can't financially support themselves. Sometimes they are risking homelessness and poverty if they don't accept the money. However, if survivors do accept the money, they are once again tied to the cult. What they learn at these desperate hours is that the cult is the one that will bail them out.

BREAKING FREE: A WORD TO SURVIVORS

It is never too late to break free of the cult. If you are a survivor, you may feel deep fear, shame, and grief at your current abuse, but you must remember your own victimization. You are not alone. Today, many survivors around the country are also attempting to remember and break free. No person is so bad, or so horrible, that he or she is unworthy of being free from that life of pain. Today there are ways out. Making the break begins with believing in yourself and seeing your own victimization. You need to remember your own childhood innocence.

If you have always been aware of your current cult involvement, you too must remember your own victimization. Every day you know the painful truth of how your life is controlled by something you cannot change. You need a place to turn. You need to find help.

Feeling Safe

I would like to share with you some techniques I used to make myself feel safe as I remembered the abuse. One important thing I did was allow my personalities to help me. My personalities wrote me a note, telling me what would happen if I let them emerge and remember:

- You will start having nightmares.
- You will want to kill yourself.
- You will want to kill other people.
- You won't want to go through it alone.
- You will want to go back to your home state.
- You will want to go back to the cult.
- You will want to kill your parents.
- You will want to start drawing your memories again.
- You will be able to work because you will feel alive and real.

The personalities also had some suggestions about how I could keep functioning despite the memories. They said:

1. Take care of yourself. Buy some bubble bath, maybe some tea. Listen to what your babies say they need. Do they want play dough? Do they want to listen to a certain type of music? Try to find those inner children. They can give you strength.

2. Keep a list of support resources by the bed. [This is the most difficult plan to implement. My parts don't trust many people. Nevertheless, next to my bed I keep the number of three friends and a few rape crisis teams that I know are educated on ritual abuse.]

3. Keep only safe knives in the house.

4. Keep all suicidal utensils out of the house, so you would have to go buy something if you wanted to kill yourself. [Stepping out of the apartment would probably make me switch out of the personality who wanted to do it.]

5. Make us enough money so we don't have to always worry about that.

6. Keep things organized in the house.

7. Let me feel, even if it is bizarre and perverted. Be willing to feel strange.

8. The adult parts have to take care of our survival needs. They must get groceries, go to the bank, and get our mail. They

must make sure we eat. They need to figure out our cash input and output. They need to make sure we go to work with a few sick days' leeway for bad memories.

I knew that remembering the abuse was more than letting myself cry about it. I knew I would have to allow myself to feel intense physical discomfort from the body memories for days. At the same time, I also had to make sure some personality went to work so we wouldn't end up out on the streets. Most important, when I felt I was in danger from my abusers, I had to take action to protect myself.

It has been over a year since I have faced my abusers. They have made a few more attempts to get me back, all unsuccessful because I listened to my personalities and took care of myself. Each day of freedom is one more step away from them toward my own life. I never thought I could feel angry at them. I always thought a part of me would always feel loyal to them. I can't express to you how wonderful it is to know they are responsible for my pain and to feel appropriately furious with them. In every cell of my body, I know they lied to me and manipulated me to get what they wanted at my expense. They stole from me the most important things in my life, the people I love. And more than ever, I know they are wrong! And I give all credit of my clear thinking to the fact that I got out. When they are still there, able to tell you how to think, feel, and breathe, there is no room for your true feelings to emerge. Freedom gives you back your mind and feelings. I am proof that you *can* get your life back. Believe in yourself: You deserve choice, freedom, and happiness. There is hope and a way out!

Chapter 8

Survivor Revictimization and Proposed Solutions

One of the most important aspects of talking about survivor revictimization is identifying the victimizers. Are they the cult members or part of the noncult public? If revictimizers are cult members, then they victimize survivors either because they are acting on orders, or because they can't handle their own entrapment in the cult. The noncult public revictimizes survivors because they don't believe survivors. They don't want to hear about ritual abuse because it scares them. They want to believe they live in a safe world. They want to send their children to school and church worry-free. They don't want to know about the corruption. They don't want to believe cults have power because they would have to change their entire understanding of the world.

When I first remembered the abuse, I told everyone about my memories. It never occurred to me that I wouldn't be believed. It never occurred to me that people wouldn't have compassion for me. Many of my friends said they believed something bad had happened to me, but they didn't believe the ritual abuse memories. A few of my friends believed the ritual abuse memories, but they couldn't believe the prevalence of the problem. It is devastating to have the memories questioned. Let's put it this way: When I am feeling the pain of the abuse and someone has the nerve to doubt my memories, it feels like I am lying there, with bruises up and down my thighs, welts on my rectum and vagina, while the onlookers determine whether I have a right to my pain.

Just as devastating as the nonbelievers were the people who believed me, but who decided I was somehow responsible for what happened. I was judged and blamed for things I couldn't control. One friend told me she didn't think I felt guilty enough. She wanted me to scream and cry in remorse for the violence I was forced to commit. What she didn't realize is that I felt so guilty when it happened that I stopped feeling at all. I don't accept blame for what happened to me. I remember how bad it was, and that the society that is judging me today is the same society that turned its back on me when I was a child.

Then there were the people who believed me, but who wanted to control my recovery. They wanted to tell me where my wounds were. They wanted to tell me how to heal. Like the cult, they told me who to love and who to hate. Not being believed is painful enough. Being blamed for what happened felt as cruel as cult behavior. Trying to tell me how to live my life, and how to understand the ritual abuse, is every bit as violating as being blamed and not believed.

Society needs to accept that sometimes people do hurt other people on purpose. They need to stop pretending they live in a safe world at the expense of those who are victimized. They need to feel their own pain so that they can have compassion for those of us who have the courage to face our pasts. And if they can't handle it, they need to understand that it is their problem, not ours.

It seems clear from the newspaper reports I have seen linking child molesting with "Satanic Rituals," that the phenomenology of the Salem witch trials is being created all over again; that is, innocent adults are being accused by hysterical children.

Catholic theologian Aidan Kelly[1]

Jeffrey Burton Russell, a historian at U.C. Santa Barbara who has written a four-volume study of the idea of the devil, sees a parallel between fear of satanism and the witch trials of the past "brought on by hysteria." . . . "My one wish is people would play this down and it will go away."

Los Angeles Times, *April 23, 1991*

Not only does the general public offer no support to survivors, many of the people who are supposed to help them don't either.

Many survivors are revictimized as they search for therapists. Most therapists do not believe children are abused in cults. Some therapists believe ritual abuse happens, but they are unaware of the prevalence of the problem. When survivors do find therapists who believe them, skeptics say survivors are led by these therapists to believe they are ritual abuse survivors. They say being a satanic ritual abuse survivor is a fad.

> Authorities say America is witnessing an epidemic of concern over Satan and his minions, especially among adherents of fundamentalist Christianity. So-called ritual abuse is only a part of it. But are these tales of incest and human sacrifice true? Many mental health experts think not.
>
> Los Angeles Times, *April 23, 1991*

When ritual abuse is publicly denied, it is extremely painful for the victims who are trying to recover. Ritual abuse survivors really have two perpetrators: the cults that violated them, and the society that let it happen and that today still does not provide them with protection and compassion. Survivors who share their cult memories are often blamed, looked down on, or not believed. Three women in this study were told they were possessed when they revealed their ritual abuse histories. One survivor said that someone accused her of being in a cult today, and the person reported her to the police. She wrote:

> Sometimes I just hate myself because there aren't a lot of people I can relate to that have experienced the same things that I have. I just hate being a cult survivor. It is so lonely. I am a "freak" in society. Everyone is cautious about making friends with me. One woman in a support group was afraid that my cult might get her. The terror society has around satanism is quite intense. I'm glad I'm a multiple. Sometimes the only safe place I have is within my inner worlds.

Another survivor in the study says,

> You cannot tell anyone in this society unless they have been abused themselves. You're looked down on. We as a

society are a long way from understanding child abuse let
alone ritual abuse . . . Once a victim, always a victim, until we
can have a voice.

Survivors are not only victimized by the attitude our society
has toward people who were abused, but they are also victimized by
clergy and psychiatrists. Survivors said the following:

> I went to a psychiatrist because I was feeling depressed,
> and began discussing my childhood. He made statements
> such as "a trauma occurs, and then children fantasize about
> the extent of what occurred." I felt completely discounted
> and it made me extremely fearful of discussing it further,
> since I was sure no one would believe me. That incident,
> along with others, was detrimental to my recovery.

> I was given an exorcism by the Catholic church. I don't
> have evil entities inside of me—I have multiple personalities!
> This caused further splitting.

Our society has a long history of victimizing people labeled
with psychiatric disorders. In the sixteenth, seventeenth, and eighteenth centuries, those designated as mentally ill were locked up in
"lunatic asylums," chained, beaten, and only fed enough food to
keep them alive. They were on display for visitors, as animals are on
display in the zoo.[2] One survivor writes:

> I feel that these people will always have power and
> anonymity because the things they do are so bizarre and
> terrible. And since there are no bodies or evidence for proof,
> society will never believe it does or could exist. We are the
> survivors, but still the victims because people want and need
> absolute proof. Therefore we remain in hiding trying to heal
> and recover alone. It's like being a prisoner of war in a war
> camp, but nobody believes it ever existed!

> I have not yet been able to work because of the intense
> memories. I am now seeking employment and have to
> explain eight months without a job. I can't say "I was
> experiencing repressed memories of ritual abuse," so I'll have
> to lie. It's been an extreme financial hardship. Therapy costs

are enormous, and I had a hard time even finding a therapy group. Most therapists in the [San Francisco] Bay Area seem to be pretty enlightened about ritual abuse; however, there are only *two* therapy groups (that I could find). When I was looking for a group, I was told by a therapist of a women's incest-survivors group that I wouldn't "fit in" and would freak out the other survivors because of the nature of my abuse. I feel all of this has been further victimizing to me. Also, I've been in and out of therapy since I was sixteen, and only now have I found a therapist who understands. . . . Society is in almost total denial about ritual abuse, and the resources for survivors just are not in place.

Most cult survivors learned not to feel their pain. In order to financially support themselves, they develop multiple personalities that help them conform to the expectations of those around them. When survivors allow themselves to feel the pain from the abuse, they are unable to participate in their daily routine for a significant length of time.

Some survivors never learn to effectively dissociate from the pain of the abuse. They have never been able to function in society. These survivors have been in and out of psychiatric hospitals for most of their lives. They may end up on the streets or on welfare. One therapist I know refers to such people as "professional multiples." Many people have little compassion or support for those who have the courage to endure the truth of their pasts—a truth that naturally encompasses pain. In our society, no matter what the excuse emotionally, if you are unable to support yourself financially, you are judged as a failure. Emotional upheaval is not accepted as an excuse for financial hardship.

Going to the Police

Survivors in this study who reported the ritual abuse to the police received a variety of responses from the officers. One survivor said she went to the police after having just experienced a "rape with burns, torture, times three with evidence. They disregarded it . . ." On the other hand, another woman reported a series of death threats left on her answering machine, and the officers took her seriously. They believed her when she told them the threats were cult-related, and they taught her ways to protect herself. Whether officers believe survivors depends on the department's attitude toward ritual abuse and on the individual who took the report. Some police departments are educated about ritual abuse; others are not. Some police officers are compassionate and helpful; others treat victims with disrespect.

Only 18 percent of the survivors in this study reported the ritual abuse to the police. Some survivors feared that cult members were in the police force. One survivor said her father's friends who abused her were judges and the district attorney. Another survivor reported that her uncle and his brother, both reported as perpetrators of her ritual abuse, are police officers.

Survivors were also afraid that reporting the abuse to the police would make them look foolish. Some survivors have self-destructive pasts and are afraid police officers would point to these chaotic instances in their lives as proof that they should not be believed. Police officers are supposed to protect the public. Survivors who seek protection should not be interrogated as if they had committed a crime. Survivors have a right to be taken seriously by police officers and by our legal system.

Survivors who speak out say they do so to take a stand against the cruelty and violence in the cults. One survivor who reported the abuse to the police said:

> My son recently disclosed in therapy that my parents had abused him in some way. I felt I was strong enough to stand up and tell.

Another woman reported the abuse to the police because:

> I believe we survivors can do more damage to their criminal activities and networkings than anyone else. We *know* more. I hate knowing there are children being horribly abused or murdered. I *have* to do something about this. *Who else will?*

Other women who do not trust the police have written books or given public-awareness talks on ritual abuse. One survivor who speaks openly about her abuse said:

There is no longer any reason why I would not talk about what happened to me.

Another survivor said:

I talk more openly, since I believe ritual abuse needs to be known about. I probably take risks doing so, but it gives me someplace to put my rage. I don't talk if I suspect someone is a perpetrator or an unsafe person.

Each survivor must decide how much and with whom they want to share their memories. Survivors have a right to talk about the abuse without being revictimized. Survivors also have a right to remain silent if they don't feel safe. They have the right to protect themselves from being hurt by people who don't believe them.

Fear of the Cult

Another reason society hears little about ritual abuse is because many victims are silenced by threats. Survivors justifiably worry that if they tell people about the abuse, then the groups may harm them or the people they love. Fifty-eight percent of the survivors in this study said they don't feel safe from their abusers today. One woman who was abused well into her thirties said that the group still watches her.

The hierarchy has a person keeping tabs on me. The less they know, the safer my family and I will be.

She selectively shares the ritual abuse only with the people she trusts. Another survivor also spoke in detail about her fears:

Even if there were more understanding I still wouldn't broadcast it because . . . I don't want cult people being told, "Hey, I found one. Let's go get her," and their trying to use me. I have enough problems with my cult and others in cults who are trained to spot people like me. It takes them time to figure it out, and I have no intention of making it easy on them.

Although some survivors in the study felt comfortable with support groups specifically for ritual abuse survivors, other people said they were afraid to attend support groups. Some survivors said that in groups specifically for ritual abuse survivors, the dynamics of the support group started to feel similar to the dynamics of cults. Some survivors said they met people at support groups who tried to pull them back into cults. Survivors not only have to worry about finding a group that allows them to tell the truth of their pasts, but they also have to worry about meeting cult members who will access them.

Surviving on a Daily Basis

In the cults, each child is made to feel like a misfit. Each child is at some point isolated, ostracized, and hurt. Children are ganged up on and emotionally and physically tormented. There is no sense of justice. It is the people who don't hurt others, the ones who are vulnerable, who are attacked.

In mainstream society, we see a similar pattern of attacking those who are vulnerable. Usually, the person who is attacked has been deemed a social misfit. Most of the time these "misfits" have done nothing to hurt other people. They are used as the scapegoats for other people's aggression and insecurities. Think of the overweight woman, the poor dresser, the nerd in grade school who was teased maliciously. The misfits who are ganged up on are usually those who can't stand up for themselves. They are the people with no friends, who hurt so badly from the attacks that they are unable to take effective action to rebuff the cruelty.

Seeing victimization in society reminds survivors of the abusive cults. Sometimes survivors wake up in the morning and don't want to get out of bed. They fear going out into the world, where they have to wear a shield of armor that is not all-protecting.

Survivors are keenly aware of the following types of victimizations that occur on a regular basis in our society. These types of victimizations remind survivors of the ritual abuse:

- shaming people who are socially inappropriate
- having to witness the mistreatment of a child

- intentionally leaving someone out of a group
- using condescending, judgmental, or critical tones or labels
- exploiting people for sexual gratification or money
- telling people not to feel or what to feel

We each witness, participate in, or are on the receiving end of these types of behavior every day. These behaviors are not as cruel as ritual abuse; but when survivors are hurt in these ways, the repressed pain from the ritual abuse emerges. We cannot shelter ourselves completely from victimizing behavior. However, we can decrease the pain victimizing behavior causes us by realizing how the victimization reminds us of times when we were severely abused.

In the case of ritual abuse survivors, when survivors are unaware of their pasts and haven't felt their repressed pain, their minds are unable to separate past from the present. When they hear a baby cry, they unconsciously start to feel the grief they felt as they watched a child tortured or killed in the cult. Survivors who are healing allow themselves to release their pain while remembering the abuse scene.

Victimized people have a choice. They can choose to protect themselves from the cruelty of others. They can accept that there are people in the world who will take advantage of them. They can learn to hide their feelings from certain people who may hurt them. If they so choose, they can conform just to get by. Taking such action should be viewed as an inconvenience, a result of living in an unsafe world. Not taking action to protect themselves up to this point should not be viewed as a personal flaw. People should not look down on survivors or criticize them because the ritual abuse left them as vulnerable as children. They no more asked for their victimizations than children ask for theirs.

PROPOSED SOLUTIONS

Professionals in law enforcement and psychology need to be educated about ritual abuse. Survivors need supportive people in their lives who believe them and who do not blame them for the abuse. They need to know that our society as a whole supports them and wants them to seek help. They need to be reminded that they are not to blame for what happened to them, and they no longer have to feel ashamed. They no longer need to hide their pain.

Therapy for Survivors

Survivors need affordable therapy. When survivors feel a memory surfacing, they need to know there is a safe place to go. Support centers must be available to adults with MPD and posttraumatic stress disorder. These centers should be designed to provide survivors with support while helping them work through their memories. Counselors should be available on a walk-in basis and by appointment. Such centers must be safe from cult infiltration. Survivors also need overnight centers where they can turn for emotional support when their memories are too overwhelming to process in a single day.

Public Outcry

Our society denies ritual abuse because acknowledging it forces us to take action. Most of us cannot live with the knowledge that we allow people to suffer. We want to be able to help. We want to be able to make a difference. Public outcry is the most influential force in this country. Support the people who come forward to speak the voice of the wounded child. Don't deny it. Do what you can in your own corner of the world to make the world a safer place. Violence and vindictive judgment is not what will stop ritual abuse. Violence is what caused ritual abuse in the first place. Only worldwide programs to protect and empower children will stop ritual abuse.

Is It Discipline or Abuse?

Our country has a difficult time upholding the laws against child abuse because we are confused about the difference between discipline and physical abuse. Discipline is supposed to benefit children. It teaches them self-control. Abuse, on the other hand, occurs when adults misuse their power in ways that violate children. Physical child abuse is legally defined as any assault against a child that leaves a mark. Under the guise of discipline, many parents have broken this law.

Education

Children need to know their rights. They need to know adults do not have a free license to do whatever they like with them. Children need to be aware that acts such as beating children, confining children in small places, and molesting children are all against the law. Children need to be encouraged to tell someone if adults are breaking the "rules." A good first step might be a mandatory video describing what is abuse that is shown in schools annually. The message needs to be clear: This country does not support violence against children. Children who are being abused must know that there are people in this world who care about them and want to help.

All people who come in contact with children should be formally educated on the symptoms of child abuse. In order to standardize reporting practices, professionals working with children could use a standard form any time they see a child who shows symptoms of abuse. Each symptom of abuse could have a point value. For example, a physical mark explained by a sketchy story could have a high point value; class disruptiveness could have a lower point value. When the point total reached a certain number, the professionals would be required by law to file a report. Such a form would need to be reviewed periodically to ensure its reliability and validity.

Therapy for Abusers

People convicted of child abuse must be required by law to attend long-term therapy. That is the only way the cycle will be stopped. The therapy must be structured to confront the following topics. First, abusers must be forced to listen to the perspective of victims. They must be required to face adult survivors expressing their feelings of rage about how their lives were stolen from them by their abusers. The abusers must see the pain their acts have caused victims.

Second, the abuser and his or her therapist must talk about how the abuse has and will adversely affect the abuser's victims: The abuser must not be allowed to dissociate from the physical and emotional pain he or she caused another human being.

Third, therapist and client need to address the abuser's childhood, which was probably filled with trauma and abuse. Through this process, abusers learn that they were vulnerable as children and that their own abuse has caused them the problems they are having today, the greatest of which is their abusive patterns.

Therapy should also address any current life problems that may be causing stress. Abusers attack children for the same reasons alcoholics take a drink: to avoid painful emotions. Confronting current problems helps the abuser minimize that stress.

Finally, abusers must learn skills that will help them change their lives. They need to learn how to redirect their abusive impulses and how to begin to be in healthy relationships.

Our country must provide abused children with protection and support. In order to protect children from abuse, we must have a system that truly protects them and empowers them toward healing.

CONCLUSION

Most of the people in violent cults were probably raised in them and are unable to get out due to trauma or amnesia. The adults who want to leave need a way out. The adults who don't want to leave need to be forced out.

If we actively attack the problem of child abuse, we actively attack the cults. The cult abusers of tomorrow are the abused children who yearn for our help today. If we protect them, we stop the cycle of ritual abuse.

NOTES

1. Quoted in Arthur Lyons, *Satan Wants You* (New York: The Mysterious Press), 160.
2. B. R. Hergenhahn, *An Introduction to the History of Psychology* (Belmont, CA: Wadsworth, 1986), 319–20.

Appendix A

The Questionnaire

1. What is your gender?
2. What is your age and occupation?
3. Please circle in which social class you were raised.
   a. upper class
   b. upper-middle class
   c. middle class
   d. working class
   e. lower class

4. Please circle in which of the following racial categories you would place yourself.
   a. Asian
   b. Afro-American
   c. Latin/Hispanic
   d. Native American
   e. White
   f. other

5. Please circle in which religion you were formally raised.
   a. Protestant
   b. Catholic
   c. Jewish
   d. Mormon
   e. Buddhist
   f. Moslem
   g. agnostic
   h. atheist
   i. other

Please answer the following questions to the best of your knowledge. If you do not know the answer to the question being asked, please write Do Not Know.

6. At what age did the ritual abuse begin?

7. At what age did the ritual abuse end?

8. How often did the ritual abuse occur?
   a. daily
   b. weekly
   c. monthly without a clear pattern
   d. only on satanic, Christian, or occult holidays
   e. I was ritually abused less than three times.
   f. other

9. Please list the locations where the ritual abuse occurred.
   a. state(s) (if you were abused outside the U.S., please indicate the country as well).
   b. Specific Locations (i.e. at home, in a church, the mountains, etc.)

10. To the best of your knowledge please list the primary person or persons that ritually abused you and their corresponding occupations. Please use no names. Just titles such as father, teacher, etc.

11. Were you ritually abused by a group of people? If yes answer the following three questions.

11a. Were you abused by more than one group of people? If yes, how many groups?

11b. Approximately how many people were involved in the group(s) that abused you?

11c. Please give us any information about the group(s) that you feel comfortable to share—purposes of rituals—organizations or roles within group—involvement in drug trafficking or child pornography—Why do you believe people get involved in these cults?—other

12. Was there an identifiable perversion of a mainstream religion or a specific religious theme used in the rituals? If yes please describe below.

13. To the best of your knowledge, were any of your perpetrators members of a secret society or a fraternal organization? If yes, please indicate the perpetrator (without using their name) and the name of the secret society or the fraternal order.

14. Please circle the form(s) of abuse that were done to you.
    a. molestation or intercourse
    b. sodomy
    c. group sex with adults
    d. child pornography
    e. child prostitution
    f. torture of you
    g. forced to torture others
    h. breeding children that were later sacrificed by the group
    i. sacrifice of animals
    j. sacrifice of humans
    k. cannibalism
    l. being drugged during the abuse
    m. other (please describe)

15. Please list the things that you knew at the time or that you found out later that helped you believe your memories of the ritual abuse. (Include verification by other family members, unexplainable physical scars, body memories, unexplainable intense emotions or any other thing you consider to be validation.)

16. Did you always remember the ritual abuse? If no please answer the following two questions.

16a. At what age did you have your first ritual abuse memory?

16b. Reflecting back upon the time period when you did *not* remember the ritual abuse, were there any clues or indicators that may have suggested you had been ritually abused as a child?

17. Please explain in detail the process of having a memory. (Please focus on the emotions and physical sensations you experience rather than the details of the memory.)

18. Please check the following people that you *do* share your ritual abuse experience with.
    a. your family of origin
    b. your closest friends
    c. your nonintimate friends
    d. your co-workers or acquaintances
    e. your therapist

19. What are the reasons you may choose *not* to share your experience of being ritually abused?

20. Have you reported any of these crimes to the police? Why or why not?

21. Do you feel safe from your abusers now?

22. Were you told you would be physically harmed if you ever talked about the abuse?

23. Do you feel as if the lack of knowledge about ritual abuse in society has affected your recovery? If yes, please give an example and describe it below.

Appendix B

Similarities in the Lives of Ritual Abuse Survivors

Question 15 in this study (see Appendix A) asked survivors to note any clues or indicators in their lives that may have suggested they were ritually abused as a child. The lists below organize these responses into meaningful categories.

Indicators Associated with Spiritual Abuse

- Vague sense of bad pain or evil when Satan was brought up
- Belief that I was evil
- Completely believing I caused people to be evil
- Believing death is a celebration
- Anger and mistrust of Christians
- Always felt like church symbols were loaded with hidden meanings
- Left church at thirteen
- Fear of God
- Strong need for a spiritual path

Indicators Associated with Dissociation

- Felt like I would die and not know a huge part of my life
- Belief as a child that there was something inside of me

- Always felt that something horrible had happened to me, but I didn't know what it was
- Always felt that there was something very, very wrong
- Always felt like there was something I needed to tell, but I couldn't remember what it was
- Felt haunted by images. Knew there was something below the surface I couldn't get at
- Knowledge of occult material I don't remember learning
- Voices chanting strange languages in my memories
- Talked to myself as "you": "You need to do your homework. You need to sleep."
- In grade school I was put in a trance and a part came up and said to everyone, "You will never get her back. She's mine now."
- Dreams, then I would wake up paralyzed and think an evil demon was trying to get inside my body
- Daydreaming of being in a traumatic situation and what I would do to get out of it
- Sister and I hated parents, but didn't know why
- Fact I could remember very little about my childhood
- Multiple Personality Disorder
- No memory of early childhood or early adulthood
- Lost time
- Lived in a self-made fantasy world most of my life
- Felt like I didn't exist. That I wasn't real
- Feeling cut off, dead inside, like I wasn't there
- Lack of pain sensation. Could break my arm and not feel it
- Ongoing body memories (with no physical cause)

Suicide Ideation or Suicide Attempts
- Suicide ideation in childhood
- Tried to kill myself several times as a child

- Suicidal most of my life
- When I stopped and went inside, I would hear, "I want to die. I want to die," or I would hear men's voices say, "No one will ever love you. Look at you. You're disgusting. You're nasty."
- Setting up my own murder
- Suicide ideation
- Suicide attempt in a trancelike state after revealing about a molestation
- Obsession with suicide that comes from outside self
- Wanting to die and not knowing why
- Attempting suicide without telling anyone, and not knowing why I was doing it
- Believing I didn't deserve to live
- Suicide attempts

Indicators Associated with Sexuality and Intimacy

As a Child

- Trying to have sex with our dog when I was five
- Heard how ritually abused children act out with pets. That was the clincher for me
- Often wet pants when playing as a child

As an Adult

- Belief that if I loved anyone, they would be tortured or killed
- Having images of torture and murder when kissed
- Needed to have arms above head during sex (like tied)
- Knowing my touch was poisonous
- Intense feelings around abortion, miscarriages, and the birth of children
- Relationships with extremely abusive partners
- Affairs with men much older than me
- Earlier in life I was a nun, and then later a prostitute

- Had to smoke pot or overeat in order to make love to my partner
- Was ashamed of my body
- Sexual dysfunction
- Sexual fear, but fascination
- Sex at thirteen with a twenty-year-old man
- Not wanting to be touched

Acting Out the Abuse in Childhood

- Obsession with sex and violence when I was a kid
- Always had remembered having my cousin whip me with a belt when I was eight and getting really sexually excited
- Acting out mutilations with my toys as a child
- Preoccupation with drawing five- and six-pointed stars when I was bored at school
- Melted red crayon on my hands to show my mom I was bleeding

Medical Problems Associated with a Ritual Abuse History

- My groin muscles were ripped in first grade by the cult, and I couldn't walk for a month and had to miss school. My mom says I did it in gymnastics
- Had infections at four that kept coming back. Had herpes, but had never had sex?
- Evidence of childbearing at twelve
- Extreme vomiting during PMS and pregnancies. Doctor asked if I had been sexually abused as a child
- Continual vaginal infections
- Rectal bleeding
- Remember internal exams when I was nine or ten
- Damage to muscles in the pelvic area
- Body scars that I didn't know where they came from

- Unexplainable urinary and vaginal infections
- Vaginal damage

Reactions to Objects That Trigger Memories

- Always afraid at Halloween
- Severe phobias of blood, bugs, death and darkness, movie lights, etc.
- Unusual fears of churches, ritual behaviors, medical procedures, being put in water, men drinking, or being passed around by men
- Overwhelming emotions on holidays
- Strong attraction to occult material
- Preference for red meat
- Hated red meat. I have been a vegetarian since I was a child
- Fascinated by gems, prisms, crystals, etc.
- Fixation on knives

  fear of

Feelings Associated with Animals

- Oversensitized and identified a lot with homeless tortured animals
- Felt protective of animals
- An intense reaction to dead animals

Indicators Associated with Being Abused by Groups

- Dreams of being chased by a group of men that were trying to kill me
- Deep belief that I had failed (that I was supposed to die a public death and had failed)
- Afraid in large groups
- Uncomfortable in groups
- Extreme self-consciousness in public places
- Always had to be in charge or performing

Indicators from Childhood or Adult Feelings

- I used to have panic attacks where I couldn't breathe and I used to say, "Oh my God. I've got to get out of here. I've got to run. Please, somebody, help me!"
- Always liked hospice nursing. I felt comfortable around dead or dying people
- Horrible nightmares about the abuse almost every night of my life
- Felt like I was going crazy
- Felt alienated
- Daily terror
- Always frightened and insecure
- Terrified by normal life events: I couldn't cope with life
- Fear of the dark
- Severe depression
- Hated having my picture taken
- Attraction to posttraumatic stress disorder movies
- Exaggerated startle response

Indicators from Childhood or Adult Behavior

- Decided I would never go to the bathroom, and that lasted for a while
- Very withdrawn
- Banged my head a lot
- Ran away from home
- School attendance was poor
- Socially was very young for my age
- Slow speech development
- Slept with a knife under my mattress
- Threw up a lot
- Would never allow myself to vomit

- Quiet, compliant, no affect
- Rarely cry
- Complete inability to trust
- Always in a crisis of some sort
- Sleepwalking
- Extreme shyness and inability to relate to peers
- No sense of physical, emotional, mental, or sexual boundaries
- Jumped from job to job
- Reckless driving

Feelings Associated with Family of Origin

- Brother's suicide and comments about Satan
- Fear of parents
- No commonality with siblings
- Very protective of the perfect parent image

Noted Addictions or Disorders

- Workaholism to avoid memories
- Drug and alcohol abuse
- Drinking problem
- Drug and alcohol addiction at fourteen
- Lifelong eating disorder
- Overeating
- Bulimia
- Anorexia
- Lifelong sleeping disorder
- Addicted to book reading
- Horrible codependency issues

Appendix C

Forms of Abuse

The following list of abuses perpetrated against survivors of ritual abuse was recorded from answers to question 14 of the questionnaire (see Appendix A), which asked the survivor, "What specifically was done to you?"

Important Note: The following information is extremely detailed and graphic and may cause intense emotions. Please read the information with great caution.

Hypnotism and Programming

- Forced to memorize cult gibberish
- Hypnotized after being drugged and given electric shock
- Trickery
- Made to feel responsible for the things that happened
- Attended cult school to learn cult philosophy

Threats

- Threats they'd get my brothers and family
- Threats of further abuse
- Told if I didn't behave, I would be locked in a cage and murdered
- Told they would cut off my arms and legs and burn off my hair

Forced Perpetration Against Others

- Taught in my twenties how to brainwash children
- Trained to murder and dismember children, infants, and later adults
- Forced to have sex with little children
- Because of the brainwashing, etc., not able to get away from cult yet
- Forced to kill my infant sister

Forced to Watch Others Being Tortured or Killed

- Friends murdered in front of me
- Forced to watch little girl murdered
- Watched a black man tortured to death

Torture, Bondage, or Forced Isolation

- Buried alive
- Buried alive with freshly killed bodies and body parts put on me
- Burned, scalded
- Locked in a basement with rats and a child's dead body
- Torture with enemas
- Smeared with foul substances with insects in it
- Put in a hole in the ground
- Hung over a vat of blood in a harness
- Tied up, imprisonment, bondage
- Wasps put on my stomach
- Drowning
- Put in a hole with snakes
- Years of confinement and isolation
- Locked in cellar rooms for long periods of time naked
- Made to lie alone, naked, in a coffin
- Torture (but only mental and what wouldn't show!)
- Put in a trunk

Spiritual Abuse

- Being told I was unwanted and abandoned by God
- Told I was a goddess, then drugged, tortured, and hypnotized not to tell about the abuse
- Spiritual torture (being told I was crazy, or a goddess, or the second coming of Christ)

Severe Sexual Violation

- Forced to have sex with dead bodies
- Baby kittens put inside my rectum and vagina by my father
- Forced group sex with siblings
- Used in poker games as a prize
- Was given an abortion
- Objects (including snake heads) were put in my vagina
- Used in betting (Can she fuck a horse?, etc.)
- Forced to have sex with other children
- Treated by a cult doctor who told me he was sewing a snake in my vagina

Other Forms of Abuse

- Urinated on
- Rituals that involved blood and products of elimination
- Ingestion of blood, urine, and feces
- Forced to drink blood
- Use of dead bodies and skeletons
- Ritual deflowering and baptism
- Land travel to and from meetings
- Having to help discard the bodies
- Marriage to Satan
- Mock murder of me

Resources

BOOKS

The following is a list of books available to clinicians and to survivors with Multiple Personality Disorder (MPD). I do not agree with some of the current therapeutic attitudes toward individuals with MPD. I encourage people to take what they like from these books and leave the rest.

On Multiple Personality Disorder

Braun, Bennett G. *Treatment of Multiple Personality Disorder.* Washington, D.C.: American Psychiatric Press, 1986. A technical book for clinicians.

Cohen, Barry, Esther Giller, and Lynn W. *Multiple Personality Disorder from the Inside Out.* Baltimore, MD: The Sidran Press, 1991. A collection of personal accounts of individuals with multiple personality disorder. A useful book for survivors and for therapists.

Gil, Eliana. *United We Stand: A Book for People with Multiple Personalities.* Walnut Creek, CA: Launch Press, 1990. A simplistic book for survivors and others interested in multiple personalities.

Kluft, Richard. *Childhood Antecedents of Multiple Personality Disorder.* Washington, D.C.: American Psychiatric Press, 1985. A technical book for therapists.

Putnam, Frank W. *Diagnosis and Treatment of Multiple Personality Disorder.* New York: Guilford Press, 1989. A technical book for clinicians.

Ross, Colin A. *Multiple Personality Disorder: Diagnosis, Clinical Features, and Treatment.* New York: John Wiley and Sons, 1989. A technical book for clinicians.

On Ritual Abuse

Again, I do not necessarily agree with some of the following approaches to the subject of ritual abuse. However, I include these books as resources because I believe some of the information in each book is valuable.

Hudson, Pamela, L.C.S.W. *Ritual Child Abuse: Discovery, Diagnosis, and Treatment*. Saratoga, CA: R&E Publishers, 1991. This book is designed to help professionals work with children who have been ritually abused. Includes a survey of ritual abuse symptoms and abuse allegations. Available from R&E Publishers, P.O. Box 2008, Saratoga, CA 95070. Phone: (408) 866-6303.

Kahaner, Larry. *Cults That Kill*. New York: Warner Books, 1988. A book combining quotes from a variety of police officers and professionals who investigate satanic crime. Some of the book addresses allegations of ritual abuse.

Raschke, Carl. *Painted Black*. San Francisco: HarperCollins, 1990. An in-depth examination of satanism in America.

Sackeim, David K. and Susan E. Devine. *Out of Darkness*. New York: Lexington Books, 1992. Addresses in detail the therapeutic, legal, and historical issues surrounding ritual abuse.

Smith, Michelle and Larry Pazder, M.D. *Michelle Remembers*. New York: Pocket Books, 1980. A personal account of a child abused in a satanic cult, as told by the survivor and her therapist. Strong Christian focus, including the use of exorcism.

Spencer, Judith. *Suffer the Child*. New York: Pocket Books, 1989. A personal account of a child abused in a satanic cult. The book was not actually written by the survivor.

On Cult Mind Control

Galanter, Marc. *Cults: Faith, Healing and Coercion*. New York: Oxford University Press, 1989.

Hassan, Steven. *Combating Mind Control*. Rochester, VT: Park Street Press, 1988.

General: Child Abuse and Recovery

Bass, Ellen and Laura Davis. *The Courage to Heal.* New York: Harper-Collins, 2d ed., 1992. An excellent book for any person confronting sexual abuse memories from childhood. The bibliography in the 1992 edition is extensive and thorough. I encourage every survivor to get a copy of this book.

Bass, Ellen and Louise Thornton. *I Never Told Anyone.* New York: HarperCollins, 1991. Another excellent book describing the pain and betrayal experienced by incest survivors. The introduction to the book describes in detail societal influence and attitudes regarding sexual abuse. An empowering book.

Davis, Laura. *The Courage to Heal Workbook.* New York: Harper-Collins, 1990. An excellent book that helps survivors actively participate in their own healing process.

Gil, Eliana. *Outgrowing the Pain.* Walnut Creek, CA: Launch Press, 1984. A simplistic book for survivors of child abuse.

BOOKLETS AND PAPERS

On Ritual Abuse

Bottoms, L. Bette, Phillip R. Shaver, and Gail S. Goodman. *Profile of Ritualistic and Religion-Related Abuse Allegations in the United States.* A professional paper presented at the ninety-ninth annual convention of the American Psychological Association, San Francisco, CA, August 19, 1991. Researchers mailed postcards to over six thousand members of the American Psychological Association in an attempt to assess the problem of ritual abuse in America. Results are presented.

Cook, Caren. *Understanding Ritual Abuse.* This booklet is based on a study of thirty-three survivors of ritual abuse. Available from RA Project, 5431 Auburn Boulevard, #215, Sacramento, CA 95841.

Germain, Ann-Marie. Master's thesis. *Ritual Abuse: Its Effects and the Process of Recovery Using Self-Help Methods and Resources, and Focusing on the Spiritual Aspect of Damage and Recovery.* This in-depth spiritual examination of ritual abuse includes very large appendices

and bibliography and discusses at some length a connection between secret societies and ritual abuse. Ann-Marie Germain is interested in speaking with other survivors who have remembered
being abused by an ancient fraternal organization. She can be
reached at S.O.M.A., P.O. Box 1397, Decatur, GA 30031. You can obtain a copy of her thesis from University Microfilms International,
300 N. Zeeb Road, Ann Arbor, MI 48106. Phone: (800) 521-0600.

Los Angeles County Commission for Women. *Ritual Abuse: Defini-
tions, Glossary, the Use of Mind Control.* A small booklet, available for
$5.00 from Ritual Abuse Task Force, 383 Hall of Administration,
500 W. Temple Street, Los Angeles, CA 90012.

Smith, Margaret. *Children Abused in Violent Rituals: Fact or Fiction?*
This booklet is based on a research study I conducted on child victims of ritual abuse. Available from Reaching Out, 1296 E. Gibson,
#218, Woodland, CA 95776.

JOURNAL AND NEWSPAPER ARTICLES

Ritual Abuse

Associated Press. "Man Convicted of Luring Boys to Sex Rituals." *The
Raleigh (N. C.) News and Observer* (Sunday, August, 27, 1989): 30A.
Describes a case in which a man pleaded guilty to luring teenage
boys into sex rituals that mimicked Christian communion.

Baker, Sue. "Questioning Satanism in England." *The Japan Times*
(Thursday, November 15, 1990). Describes a number of ritual abuse
cases that have been reported to the police in England.

Barron, David. "Tender Witnesses, Delicate Testimony." *Raleigh
(N.C.) News and Observer* (March 31, 1991). Describes a case in
which children reported ritual abuse at their preschool.

Dew, Joe. "Johnston Couple Win Child Sex Abuse Suit." *The Raleigh
(N.C.) News and Observer* (Tuesday, March 27, 1990). Describes how
parents won a suit against a babysitter accused by their children of
molesting them and forcing them to participate in satanic rituals.

Driscoll, Lynda N. and Cheryl Wright, Ph.D. "Survivors of Childhood Ritual Abuse: Multi-generational Satanic Cult Involvement."
Treating Abuse Today (September/October 1991). This article presents

the results of an in-depth study on adult survivors of multiple generations of ritual abuse.

"Ex-Deputy Gets 20 Years." *The Oregonian* (Friday, April 6, 1990). Describes a criminal case in which a once prominent member of the community pleaded guilty to six counts of third-degree rape he said took place during satanic rituals.

Hubert, Cynthia. "Day-care Abuse Stuns Iowa Town." *Edgewood (Iowa) Daily Herald* (December 4, 1989). Describes a case in which children made allegations of ritual abuse and the defendant was convicted.

Hunt, Patricia and Margaret Baird. "Children of Sex Rings." *Child Welfare* 69, no. 3 (May-June 1990). Describes in detail the experience of children abused in sex rings and is validating and relevant to ritual abuse survivors.

"Incest: A Chilling Report." *Lear's* (February 1992). This article not only describes in detail the problem of incest, but also discusses at some length further findings regarding the McMartin Preschool case. Write to: *Lear's*, Department I, 655 Madison Avenue, New York, New York, 10021.

Jonker, F. and P. Jonker Bakker. "Experiences with Ritualist Child Sexual Abuse: A Case Study from the Netherlands." *Child Abuse and Neglect* 15 (1991): 191–96.

Journal of Child and Youth Care, Special Issue on Ritual Abuse. Available from Calgari Press, 117 Woodpark Boulevard, SW, Calgari, Alberta Canada T2W-2Z8. (403) 281-3838

Kelley, Susan J., R.N., Ph.D. "Ritual Abuse of Children: Dynamics and Impact." *Cultic Studies Journal* 5, no. 2 (1988). A good overview of the social problem of ritual abuse.

Marlin, Beth. "The Cannibal Case." *Canadian Lawyer* (October 1987). Describes in detail a case where children reported being ritually abused by their mother and her boyfriend. The article initially describes a court scene that seems to exemplify the tragedy of multigenerational ritual abuse.

"Mormons Investigating Satanic Abuse." *Boulder Daily Camera,* quoted in the *Chicago Tribune* (November 3, 1991). Describes an investigation made by the Church of Jesus Christ of Latter-day Saints of sixty cases in which Mormons described having undergone ritual abuse.

Neswald, David W., M.A., M.F.C.C., and Catherine Gould, Ph.D., "Basic Treatment and Program Neutralization Strategies for Adult MPD Survivors of Satanic Ritual Abuse." *Treating Abuse Today* 12, no. 3. This article describes useful techniques for therapists and others in regard to healing from MPD and neutralizing cult programming. The article is particularly impressive in its honest assessment of the problem of current ritual abuse reprogramming when survivors are in therapy.

Ross, A. S. "Going to Trial Despite a Questionable Probe." *San Francisco Examiner* (Sunday, September 28, 1986): A8. An article that includes ritual abuse allegations at a church.

"Satanic Storm." *Boulder (CO) Sunday Camera* (March 22, 1992): Section C. An in-depth article on satanism and ritual abuse based on a case study of a successful Denver woman.

Schindehette, Susan. "The McMartin Nightmare" *People* (February 5, 1990). The McMartin Preschool case was the first well-publicized sexual abuse case in which the victims reported elements of ritual abuse. This article summarizes some of the key points pertaining to the McMartin case.

"Sensational Cases Across the Country: Cases from the Bay Area and the West." *San Francisco Examiner* (September 28, 1986). This article presents over twenty cases around the country in which children reported elements of ritual abuse. They also noted some cases that resulted in convictions.

Snow, Barbara and Teena Sorenson. "Ritualistic Child Abuse in a Neighborhood Setting." *Journal of Interpersonal Violence* 5, no. 4 (December 1990): 474–87. This article describes some previous articles on ritual abuse not mentioned in this Resource guide, and also presents a study on similarities in ritual abuse allegations.

Tackett, Michael. "A Chilling Tale of Child Abuse No One Can Prove." *Chicago Tribune* (Friday, May 17, 1991). Describes in some detail the Evansville, Indiana, case where children reported ritual abuse at school.

"Vortex of Evil." *New Statesman and Society* (October 5, 1990): 12–14. Describes a case that took place in Nottingham, England, where children reported ritual abuse and the defendants pleaded guilty.

OCCULT, SECRET SOCIETY, AND SOCIOLOGICAL BOOKS AND ARTICLES

Crowley, Aleister. *The Book of Lies*. York Beach, ME: Samuel Weiser, 1988. Aleister Crowley was a well-known occultist, believed by some to have practiced a sexualized mass.

———. *The Confessions of Aleister Crowley*. London: Arkana, 1979. This book, written by Aleister Crowley himself, describes Crowley's own beliefs and his involvement in Masonry.

———. *The Law Is for All: An Extenuation of the Book of Law*. Las Vegas, NV: The Falcon Press, 1988. Believed by some to be the source book for the "new religion that will unite all people." Part III of the book describes practices similar to the acts described by ritual abuse survivors.

Fisher, Paul A. *Behind the Lodge Door: Church, State and Freemasonry in America*. Rockfield, IL: Tan Books and Publishers, 1991. An in-depth analysis of Masonry in America from a Christian perspective.

Hill, Sally, M.S.W., and Jean Goodwin, M.D., M.P.H. "Satanism: Similarities between Patient Accounts and Pre-Inquisition Historical Sources." *Dissociation: Progress in the Dissociative Disorders* 2, no. 1 (1989): 39–42. This article describes in detail similarities between accusations made by the Catholic church focusing on Gnosticism and memories of ritual abuse survivors.

Howard, Michael. *The Occult Conspiracy*. Rochester, VT: Destiny Books, 1989. From a supportive position of the cause of the occult, the author describes the history and modern structure of secret societies with the aim of world unification.

Kah, Gary H. *En Route to Global Occupation*. Lafayette, LA: Huntington House Publishers, 1992. This book suggests that our current government is attempting to unite the world to create a New World Order through global politics, economics, and secret control of government by wealthy, powerful people. This book is from a Christian perspective.

La Vey, Anton Szandor. *The Satanic Bible.* New York: Avon Books, 1969. Believed by some to be the "bible" for satanists.

Pike, Albert. *Morals and Dogma of the Ancient and Accepted Scottish Rite of Freemasonry.* Washington, D.C.: House of the Temple, 1966. Originally published in 1871. Describes in detail Masonic beliefs. No longer in print, but available at some libraries.

Pfohl, Stephen J. *Images of Deviance and Social Control.* New York: McGraw-Hill Publishing Company, 1985. A comprehensive book examining a number of different sociological theories in relation to deviant behavior. Chapter 2 includes graphic detail of cruelty conducted during the Inquisition, under the "Demonic Perspective" of understanding deviant behavior.

Raschke, Carl. *Painted Black.* San Francisco: HarperSanFrancisco, 1990. A well-researched examination of satanism in the United States today.

Robinson, James M., ed. *The Nag Hammadi Library.* San Francisco: Harper & Row, 1978. Provides the English translations of a number of ancient Gnostic texts that were discovered in Egypt in 1945.

Seligmann, Kurt. *The History of Magic and the Occult.* New York: Harmony Books, 1975. A book describing the beliefs of a variety of magical traditions.

Shaw, Jim and Tom McKenney. *The Deadly Deception.* Lafayette, LA: Huntington House, 1988. A book with a Christian message written by an ex-Mason who describes his experiences in Masonry.

Starhawk. *The Spiral Dance.* San Francisco: Harper & Row, 1989. Describes in detail the beliefs and practices of nonviolent witches. Illustrates that witchcraft in the United States, without the use of violence, is a very fulfilling, empowering religion for participants.

Still, William T. *New World Order: The Ancient Plan of Secret Societies.* Lafayette, LA: Huntington House Publishers, 1990. From a nonsupportive position, describes the ancient plan of secret societies to bring all nations under a one-world government. This book is from a Christian perspective.

Walker, Benjamin. *Gnosticism: Its History and Influence.* Wellingborough, Northamptonshire, England: Crucible, 1989. Describes in detail the beliefs and practices of ancient Gnosticism.

Wattson, Bruce. "Thou Shalt Not Suffer a Witch to Live." *Smithsonian* 23, no. 1 (April, 1992). An excellent overview of the cruelty associated with the Inquisition and the Salem witch trials.

AUDIOCASSETTES AND VIDEOTAPES

On Multiple Personality Disorder

Reaching Out
1296 E. Gibson Road, #218
Woodland, CA 95776

Reaching Out has a series of audiocassettes available to ritual abuse survivors, most of which address issues associated with multiple personality disorder.

Audio Transcripts, Ltd.
335 South Patrick Street
Alexandria, VA 22314
(800) 338-2111

Provides a free catalogue featuring audiocassettes from the major professional meetings on MPD and dissociation.

The Center for Dissociative Disorders
Ridgeview Institute
3995 South Cobb Drive
Smyrna, GA 30080
(800) 345-9775

Provides medical personnel and professionals with a video entitled *Multiple Personality Disorder: An Overview,* either for seven-day rental or for purchase.

On Ritual Abuse

Reaching Out
1296 E. Gibson Road, #218
Woodland, CA 95776

This ten-part series of audiocassettes provides information on child victims, programming, getting out, cult motivation, suicide and self-mutilation, support, therapy, MPD, work and relationships, and spirituality. Most of the information on the tapes does not duplicate material in this book. If interested, please request an order form from Reaching Out.

BAWAR
Healing Hearts
357 MacArthur Blvd.
Oakland, CA 94610

Has a number of audiocassettes from conferences and workshops on ritual abuse. Many of the speakers on the cassettes are survivors of ritual abuse speaking to an audience of other survivors. I strongly recommend the tape "Cooperation vs. Integration." Ask for a listing of currently available tapes.

Community Program Innovations
P.O. Box 2066
Danvers, MA 01923-5066
(508) 774-0815

In May 1991, this organization held a national conference on cults and ritualistic abuse. The audiocassettes from this conference are available to anyone who is interested. Contact the organization by phone to receive a listing of the tapes available.

NEWSLETTERS AND JOURNALS

On Multiple Personality Disorder

Reaching Out
1296 E. Gibson Road, #218
Woodland, CA 95776

Reaching Out publishes a twelve-page newsletter designed to update readers on current news and issues related to multiple personality disorder.

Dissociation: Progress in the Dissociative Disorders
The Journal of the International Society for the Study

of Multiple Personality Disorder
c/o Ridgeview Institute
3995 South Cobb Drive
Smyrna, GA 30080-6397
(800) 345-9775

A professional journal for clinicians.

Many Voices
P.O. Box 2639
Cincinnati, OH 45201-2639

A bimonthly publication for people with multiple personalities.

On Ritual Abuse

Reaching Out
1296 E. Gibson Road, #218
Woodland, CA 95776

Reaching Out publishes a ten-page newsletter the provides readers with current news and issues pertaining to ritual abuse.

Survivorship
3181 Mission Street, #139
San Francisco, CA 94110

A newsletter for ritual abuse and torture survivors.

Cultic Studies Journal
American Family Foundation
Box 336
Weston, MA 02193

A journal on cults and manipulative techniques of Social Influence.

On Child Abuse

Treating Abuse Today
David L. Calof
2722 Eastlake Avenue E.

Suite 300
Seattle, WA 98102.

A journal for professionals and survivors that includes articles on MPD and ritual abuse.

ORGANIZATIONS

Multiple Personality Disorder

Reaching Out
1296 E. Gibson Road, #218
Woodland, CA 95776

Provides audiocassettes, a newsletter, a resource guide, pen-pals, books, and financial assistance to order materials through Reaching Out.

Education/Dissociation
c/o The Muskoka Meeting Place for Counseling and Education
955 Muskoka Road South
Gravenhurst, Ontario P0C 1G0
(705) 687-7686 or (416) 274-9146

Provides educational materials and conducts conferences and workshops for professionals.

International Society for the Study of Multiple Personality
Disorder (ISSMP&D)
5700 Old Orchard Road, First Floor
Skokie, IL 60077-1024
(708) 966-4322

A professional organization for therapists who work with MPD and dissociative clients. Provides resources on study groups and on recent articles and books written on MPD. Holds an annual conference.

The Sidran Foundation
211 Southway
Baltimore, MD 21218

An organization dedicated to the advocacy, education, and re-search of individuals suffering from catastrophic induced trauma resulting in psychiatric disorders. Contact the Sidran Foundation for a copy of the *Sidran Foundation Bookshelf,* an easy-order catalogue listing a large number of books on multiple personalities and dissociation.

Ritual Abuse

Reaching Out
1296 E. Gibson Road, #218
Woodland, CA 95776

Provides audiocassettes, a newsletter, a resource guide, penpals, books, and financial assistance to order material through Reaching Out.

Believe the Children
P.O. Box 268462
Chicago IL 60626
(708) 515-5432

Believe the Children provides information and referral to survivors and their advocates and publishes a national newsletter.

Traans
P.O. Box 29064
Delamont Station
1996 West Broadway
Vancouver, B.C., Canada V6J 5C2

Voices in Action
P.O. Box 148309
Chicago, IL 60614

Information, referrals, and resources for survivors and advocates. Publishes a newsletter and conducts an annual conference.

SUPPORT GROUPS

Contact your local rape crisis team to find a support group, or ask therapists in your area who work with ritual abuse survivors. Open groups that are not run by safe facilitators may need to be avoided.

Some survivors say that violent cults attempt to infiltrate open groups.

Survivors of ritual abuse may want to contact their local rape crisis team to find out if volunteers are trained on the topic of ritual abuse. If they are trained on ritual abuse, use the twenty-four-hour hot line for support. If they are not, you may want to educate them by introducing them to audiocassettes or literature on the topic.

THERAPISTS

Reaching Out has an audiocassette called "Therapy: Finding a Therapist and Getting Your Needs Met" that can give you some good tips for finding a qualified therapist. The tape is also helpful for survivors interested in evaluating the quality of their current therapeutic relationship. You may also use the techniques in *The Courage to Heal Workbook* by Laura Davis (see listing above) to interview and assess your feelings about a potential therapist. Reaching Out also has a resource guide you can order, which lists therapists trained on ritual abuse. All therapists completed a questionnaire to determine their education and attitude toward ritual abuse. The results of the questionnaire are included in the resource guide. Please write to: Reaching Out, 1296 E. Gibson Road, #218, Woodland, CA 95776. If you are a therapist interested in being presented on this list, please contact Reaching Out as soon as possible.

You may also want to contact your local rape crisis team to get names of therapists in your area who work with incest survivors. You may choose to train a therapist on ritual abuse using audiocassettes and books.

PSYCHIATRIC HOSPITALS/TRAUMA CENTERS

Educate yourself about a particular psychiatric hospital before you check yourself into it. You are a consumer, and the hospital is providing you with a service. Ask questions about the use of medication, attitudes toward memories and abreaction, attitudes toward extreme emotion, and so on, and attempt to verify the answers by touring the ward and asking more specific questions. Remember, MPD is not a psychosis. It is a curable defense to extreme trauma.

Be cautious about taking medication for a prolonged length of time. I suggest that survivors use outpatient resources, such as therapists and rape crisis teams, for support whenever possible. A number of survivors have reported being revictimized in psychiatric hospitals.

Cottonwood de Albuquerque
804 Blythe Road
Las Lunas, NM 87031
(800) 877-4519

Cottonwood is a trauma center as opposed to a psychiatric hospital. The program is to help traumatized individuals release their pain. It is for sexual abuse survivors as well as ritual abuse survivors.

The Charter Hospital of Dallas
Dissociative Disorder Unit
6800 Preston Road
Plano, TX 75024
(800) 255-3312

Trauma and Recovery Program
Akron General Medical Center
400 Wabash Avenue
Akron, OH 44307
(216) 384-6525

The Charter Peachford Hospital
2151 Peachford Road
Atlanta, GA 30338
(800) 451-2151

Peachford has a program especially for child and adolescent MPD.